Street by Street

STEVE

BALDOCK, HITCHIN, KNEBWORTH, LETCHWORTH

Arlesey, Church End, Henlow, Ickleford, Stotfold, Walkern, Weston

1st edition August 2002

Published by AA Publishing (a trading name of Automobile Association Developments Limited, whose registered office is Millstream, Maidenhead Road, Windsor, Berkshire SL4 5GD. Registered number 1878835).

Schools address data provided by Education Direct.

One-way street data provided by:

Tele Atlas © Tele Atlas N.V.

Mapping produced by the Cartographic Department of The Automobile Association. A00965b

A CIP Catalogue record for this book is available from the British Library.

Printed by GRAFIASA S.A., Porto, Portugal

Ref: ML190

Key to map symbols ii

Key to map pages 1

Enlarged scale pages 2-3

Street by Street 4-45

Index – towns & villages 46

Index – streets 47-52

Index – featured places 52-53

Map Symbols

Junction 9

Motorway & junction

Services

Motorway service area

Primary road single/dual carriageway

Services

Primary road service area

A road single/dual carriageway

B road single/dual carriageway

Other road single/dual carriageway

Minor/private road, access may be restricted

One-way street

Pedestrian area

Track or footpath

Road under construction

Road tunnel

AA Service Centre

Parking

Park & Ride

Bus/coach station

Railway & main railway station

Railway & minor railway station

Underground station

Light railway & station

Preserved private railway

LC

Level crossing

Tramway

Ferry route

Airport runway

County, administrative boundary

Mounds

93

Page continuation 1:15,000

7

Page continuation to enlarged scale 1:10,000

River/canal, lake, pier

Aqueduct, lock, weir

465

Winter Hill

Peak (with height in metres)

Beach

Coniferous woodland

Broadleaved woodland

Mixed woodland

Park

Cemetery

Built-up area

Featured building

City wall

A&E

Hospital with 24-hour A&E department

PO

Post Office

Public library

Tourist Information Centre

Petrol station

Major suppliers only

Church/chapel

Public toilets

Toilet with disabled facilities

PH

Public house

AA recommended

Restaurant

AA inspected

Theatre or performing arts centre

Cinema

Golf course

Camping

AA inspected

Caravan site

AA inspected

Camping & caravan site

AA inspected

Theme park

Abbey, cathedral or priory

Castle

Historic house or building

Wakehurst Place NT

National Trust property

Museum or art gallery

Roman antiquity

Ancient site, battlefield or monument

Industrial interest

Garden

Arboretum

Farm or animal centre

Zoological or wildlife collection

Bird collection

Nature reserve

Visitor or heritage centre

Country park

Cave

Windmill

Distillery, brewery or vineyard

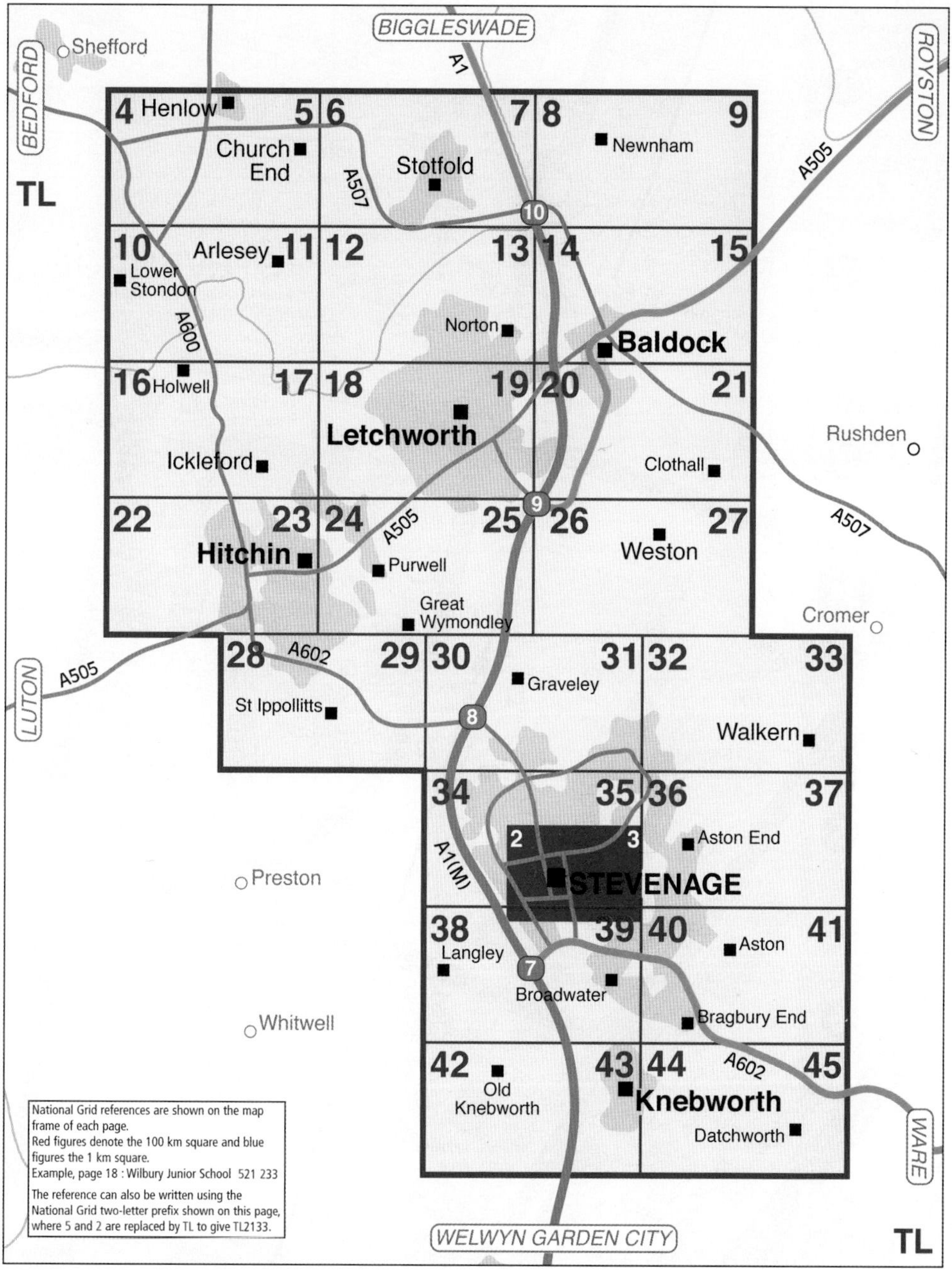

BIGGLESWADE
ROYSTON
BEDFORD
LUTON
WARE
WELWYN GARDEN CITY
TL

A1 · A1(M) · A505 · A507 · A600 · A602 · Junctions 7, 8, 9, 10

Page	Places
4 / 5	Henlow, Church End
6 / 7	Stotfold
8 / 9	Newnham
10 / 11	Arlesey, Lower Stondon
12 / 13	Norton
14 / 15	Baldock
16 / 17	Holwell, Ickleford
18 / 19	Letchworth
20 / 21	Clothall
22 / 23	Hitchin
24 / 25	Purwell, Great Wymondley
26 / 27	Weston
28 / 29	St Ippollitts
30 / 31	Graveley
32 / 33	Walkern
34 / 35	Stevenage
36 / 37	Aston End
2 / 3	Stevenage
38 / 39	Langley, Broadwater
40 / 41	Aston, Bragbury End
42 / 43	Old Knebworth, Knebworth
44 / 45	Datchworth

Outside the mapped pages: Shefford, Rushden, Cromer, Preston, Whitwell

National Grid references are shown on the map frame of each page.
Red figures denote the 100 km square and blue figures the 1 km square.
Example, page 18 : Wilbury Junior School 521 233
The reference can also be written using the National Grid two-letter prefix shown on this page, where 5 and 2 are replaced by TL to give TL2133.

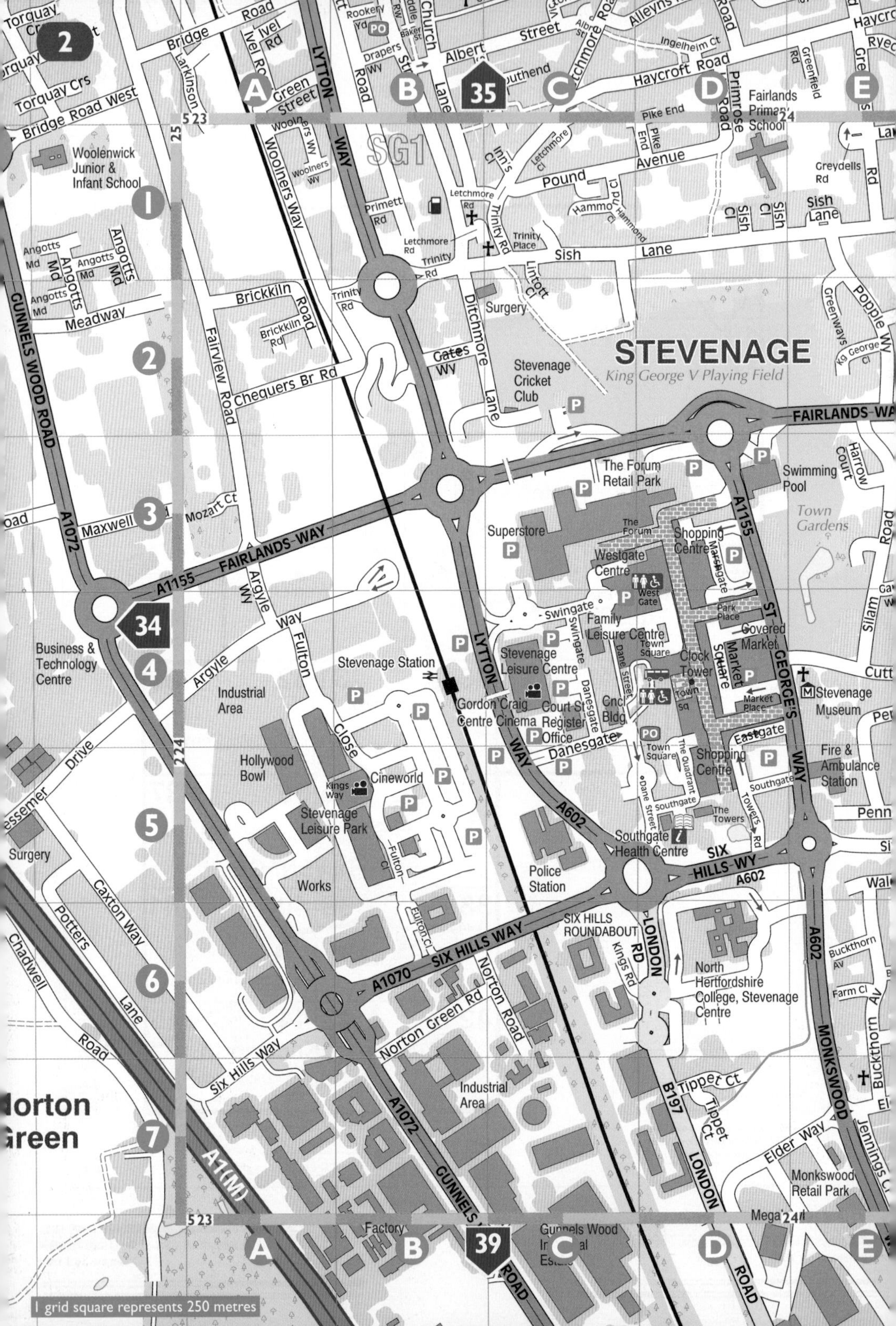
2
35
34
39
STEVENAGE
King George V Playing Field
SG1
Woolenwick Junior & Infant School
Stevenage Cricket Club
The Forum Retail Park
Swimming Pool
Town Gardens
Superstore
Westgate Centre
Shopping Centre
Family Leisure Centre
Stevenage Leisure Centre
Stevenage Station
Gordon Craig Centre
Cinema
Court St
Register Office
Cncl Bldg
Clock Tower
Covered Market
Stevenage Museum
Fire & Ambulance Station
Business & Technology Centre
Industrial Area
Hollywood Bowl
Cineworld
Stevenage Leisure Park
Works
Police Station
Southgate Health Centre
SIX HILLS ROUNDABOUT
North Hertfordshire College, Stevenage Centre
Monkswood Retail Park
Gunnels Wood Industrial Estate
Factory
Surgery
Norton Green
Fairlands Primary School
FAIRLANDS WAY
LYTTON WAY
GUNNELS WOOD ROAD
SIX HILLS WAY
ST GEORGE'S WAY
MONKSWOOD WAY
LONDON ROAD
A1(M)
A1072
A1155
A602
A1070
B197
1 grid square represents 250 metres

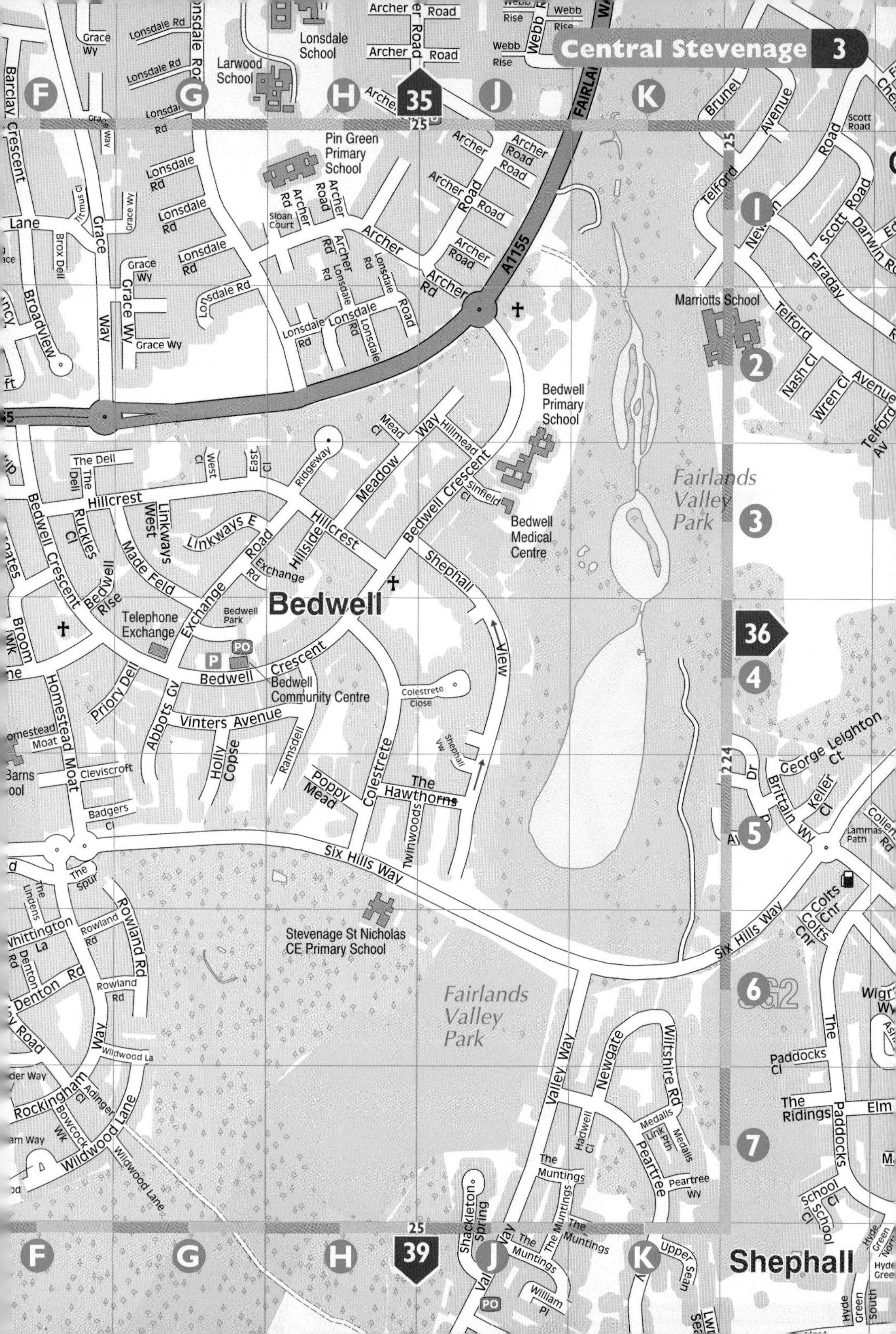
F
G
H
J
K
35
25
39
36
1
2
3
4
5
6
7
Lonsdale School
Larwood School
Pin Green Primary School
Archer Road
Webb Rise
Lonsdale Rd
Grace Wy
Grace Way
Barclay Crescent
Titmus Cl
Brox Dell
Lane
Broadview
Sloan Court
A1155
Fairlands Way
Brunel
Avenue
Telford
Newton
Scott Road
Darwin Rd
Faraday
Telford Avenue
Marriotts School
Nash Cl
Wren Cl
Telford Av
Bedwell Primary School
Fairlands Valley Park
Bedwell Medical Centre
Sinfield Cl
Hillmead
Meadow Way
Mead Cl
Ridgeway
West Cl
East Cl
The Dell
Hillcrest
Linkways West
Linkways E
Ruckles Cl
Bedwell Crescent
Made Feld
Exchange Road
Exchange Rd
Hillside
Shephall View
Bedwell
Bedwell Rise
Bedwell Park
Telephone Exchange
PO
P
Bedwell Community Centre
Broom
Homestead Moat
Priory Dell
Abbots Gv
Vinters Avenue
Holly Copse
Ramsdell
Colestrete Close
Colestrete
Shephall Vw
Cleviscroft
Badgers Cl
Poppy Mead
The Hawthorns
Twinwoods
Six Hills Way
The Spur
The Lindens
Whittington La
Rowland Rd
Denton Rd
Stevenage St Nicholas CE Primary School
Rowland Rd
Way
Wildwood La
Wildwood Lane
Rockingham
Adinger
Bowcock Wk
Valley Way
Newgate
Wiltshire Rd
Hadwell Cl
Medalls Link Pth
Medalls
Peartree
Peartree Wy
The Muntings
Shackleton Spring
William Pl
Upper Sean
George Leighton Ct
Brittain Wy
Keller Cl
Dr
Lammas Path
Collen Rd
Colts Cnr
SG2
The Paddocks
Paddocks Cl
The Ridings
Elm
School Cl
Hyde Green
Shephall

4
Samuel Whitbread
Community
College
Maple Cl
Birch Close
Bunyan Close
Knolls Way
Alexander Close
PO
Broad
The Joint
Hitchin Lane
Street
A
B
C
D
516
17
HE
New Road
Hitchin Road
Wren Park
Clifton Road
Manor Road
Westfield Road
1
38
A507
2
Hoo Farm
A600
HITCHIN ROAD
3
Business Park
Henlow Airfield
Westfield Farm
37
SG16
4
HITCHIN ROAD
BEDFORD ROAD
5
Derwent Lower School
Weedon Cl
Morris Close
Jones Close
Owen
Dawson Close
Tedder Avenue
Whitworth Jones Av
Ryley Cl
Franks
236
516
17
A
B
C
D
10
Oldfield Farm Rd
Nene Rd
Olympus Rd
Road
Derwent
Burnett
PO
Borton
Avon
Road
1 grid square represents 500 metres

HIGH STREET
Church Road
Groveside
Barn Close
Sprksfl
Henlow Middle School
The Grange
Park Lane
Coach Road
Elm Close
Oak Dr
Chs Fr
Crossways Cl
The Gdns
Arlesey Road
Park Farm Close
ARLESEY ROAD
A507
Arlesey Station
Old Oak Cl
The Limes
Vicarage Cl
The Poplars
Stotfold Road
Old Oak Close Industrial Estate
Church End
Chase Close
St Peter's Avenue
Saffron Cl
Carters Way
Glebe Avenue
House Lane
Church Lane
The Rally
Carters Close
Bury Mead
Chase Hill Rd
Church End
Manor Farm
High Street
Lewis Lane
Lymans Road
Cox's Way
Everest Cl
Blue Gold Trading Estate
Gothic Way
Hillary Rise
Lynton Av
Cluny Way
Gothic M Lower S
Health Centre
Arlesey
Cricketer's Road
St John's Rd
Primary Way
Ind Estate
Wesley Close
Old School Walk
Primrose Lane
Primrose Cl
Mill Lane
Davis' Row
Oldfield Farm
SG15
E F G H
18 19
38 37 236
1 2 3 4 5
6
11

A
B
C
D
520
21
1
38
2
Pix Ct
Stotfold Road
The Poplars
Chase Close
St Peter's Avenue
Church Lane
Glebe Avenue
House Lane
PO
Church End
3
5
Chase Farm
37
A507
Waterloo Farm
Stotfold
Road
PH
Arlesey Road
Surgery
The Gardens
Heron Way
Waters End
St Olives
High Street
Lewis Lane
4
Lymans Road
Cox's Way
Everest Cl
Gothic Way
Hillary Rise
Lynton Av
Gothic Mede Lower School
Health Centre
5
Cluny Way
Arlesey
236
Hitchin Road
Coppice Mead
Roe Close
Hazel Grove
Pix Road
Highbush Road
Hyde Avenue
Primary Way
Old School Walk
Wesley Close
SG15
12
1 grid square represents 500 metres

stwick
E
F
G
H
22
23
Mill Lane
Hinxworth Road
A1(T)
Taylor's Road
River Ivel
Calc
I
Stotfold Road
38
Taylor's Road
Works
Road
Fen End
2
Avenue
Ivel Way
Castles Close
Silverbirch Avenue
Regent Court
Road
The Green
Wrayfields
Nthr
Malthouse Lane
The Green
Street
Road
Stotfold
A1(T)
3
Radwell Grange
8
Crescent
Oliver's
Rook
PO
Regent
Mowbray Cr
Home Close
Lane
Cemetery
37
St Marys Lower School
Tree
Brayes Manor
Church
Mill
Road
Roecroft School
4
The Avenue
Alexander Road
The Crofts
Lane
Mill Close
Baldock Service Area
Church Road
Chequers Close
St Mary's Avenue
Queen Street
High
Superstore
Street
Chapel Place
Grange Drive
Works
Queen Anne's Close
Murrell Lane
Norton Road
Baldock
Road
The Coppens
Groveland Way
Littlebury Cl
A507
Junction 10
5
236
22
23
E
F
13
G
Radwell
H
Norton Road
Radwell
Lane
A1(M)
A507

A
B
C
D
524
25
Caldecote
Road
Caldecote
Road
Newnham Way
Road
Ashwell
PO
Newnham
Newnham
Road
Radwell Grange
7
Hullockpit
Hill
Baldock Service Area
Newnham Road
38
37
236
1
2
3
4
5
adwell
Lane
A1(M)
A50
14
1 grid square represents 500 metres

E
F
G
H
26
27
I
2
3
4
5
38
37
236
Icknield Way Path
The Knoll
Icknield Way Path
SG7
Ashwell Road
Cat Ditch
Icknield Way Path
Bygrave
Manor House
Ashwell Road
15

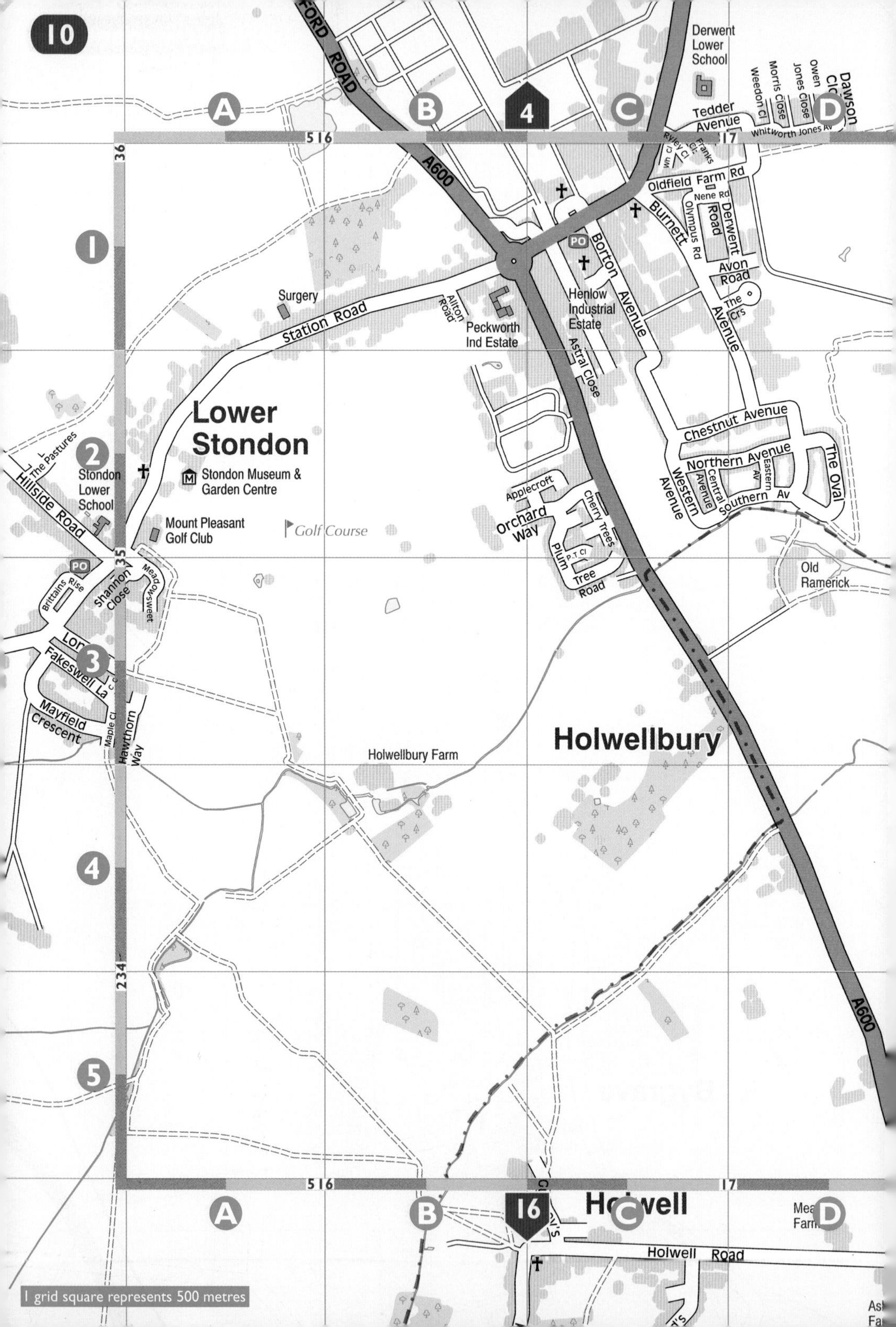

Lower Stondon
Holwellbury
Holwell
Station Road
A600
FORD ROAD
Surgery
Allton Road
Peckworth Ind Estate
Henlow Industrial Estate
Borton Avenue
Astral Close
Burnett Avenue
Derwent Road
Olympus Rd
Nene Rd
Oldfield Farm Rd
Avon Road
The Crs
Derwent Lower School
Tedder Avenue
Weedon Cl
Morris Close
Jones Close
Owen Cl
Dawson Cl
Whitworth Jones Av
Ryley Cl
Franks Cl
Chestnut Avenue
Northern Avenue
Western Avenue
Central Avenue
Eastern Av
Southern Av
The Oval
Applecroft
Orchard Way
Cherry Trees
Plum Tree Road
P.T Cl
Old Ramerick
Stondon Museum & Garden Centre
Mount Pleasant Golf Club
Golf Course
Stondon Lower School
The Pastures
Hillside Road
Britains Rise
Shannon Close
Meadowsweet
Fakeswell La
Mayfield Crescent
Maple Cl
Hawthorn Way
Holwellbury Farm
Holwell Road
PO
A
B
C
D
1
2
3
4
5
4
16
516
17
36
35
234
1 grid square represents 500 metres

Arlesey
Health Centre
Cricketer's Road
St John's Rd
Primary Way
SG15
Ind Estate
Primrose Lane
Primrose Cl
Wesley Close
Old School Walk
Mill Lane
Davis' Row
Straw Plait
Station Rd
PO
Hospital Road
West Drive
Albert Rd
Lamb Meadow
Arlesey FC
River Hiz
Hitchin Road
London Row
Oldfield Farm
Hitchin Road Industrial And Business Centre
Portland Industrial Estate
Jubilee Crescent
Ramerick Gdns
Cem
Bedfordshire County
Hertfordshire County
New Ramerwick Farm
Wilbury Farm
Pestol Farm
E
F
G
H
5
17
12
18
19
36
35
234
1
2
3
4
5

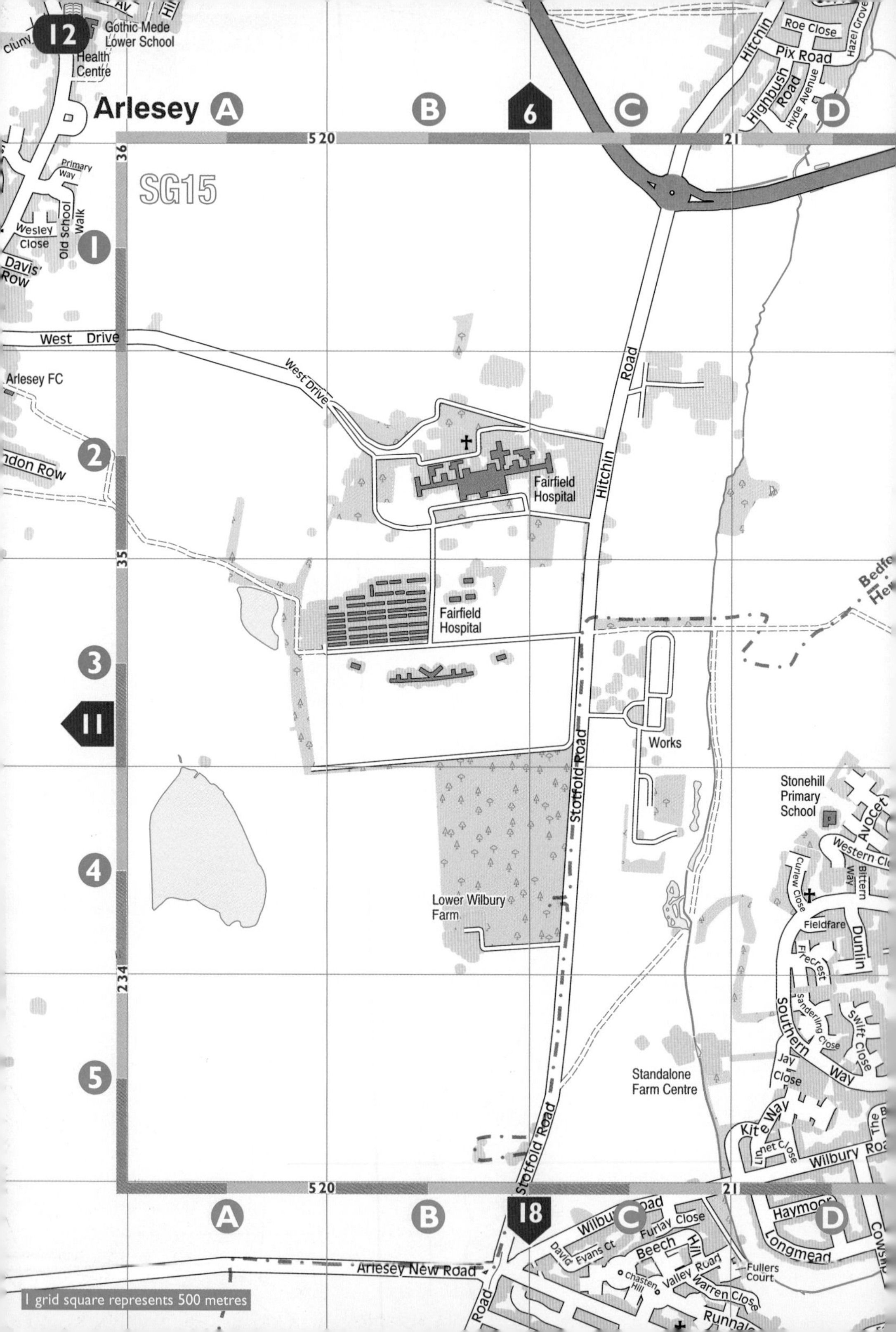
12
Gothic Mede
Lower School
Health
Centre
Arlesey
A
B
6
C
D
5 20
21
36
SG15
Primary
Way
Wesley
Close
Old School
Walk
Davis'
Row
1
Roe Close
Pix Road
Hitchin
Highbush
Road
Hyde Avenue
Hazel Grove
West Drive
West Drive
Arlesey FC
2
Road
Hitchin
Fairfield
Hospital
35
Fairfield
Hospital
3
11
Works
Stotfold Road
Stonehill
Primary
School
Avocet
Western Cl
4
Curlew Close
Bittern
Way
Lower Wilbury
Farm
Fieldfare
Dunlin
Firecrest
234
Sanderling Close
Swift Close
Southern
Way
Jay
Close
5
Standalone
Farm Centre
Stotfold Road
Kite Way
Wilbury Ro
5 20
21
A
B
18
C
D
Haymoor
Longmead
Furlay Close
David Evans Ct
Beech
Hill
Valley Road
Chasten
Hill
Warren Close
Fullers
Court
Arlesey New Road
Road
Runnalo
1 grid square represents 500 metres

Norton 13
Junction 10
Radwell
Norton
A507
A1(M)
A505
Norton Road
Radwell Lane
Norton Bury Lane
Norton Bury
River Ivel
Gaunts Way
Kimberley
Stoneley
Burley
Grange Junior School
Sparhawke
Whitehicks
Maycroft Way
Northfields
Northfields Infant School
Normans Close
Saxon Close
Ordelmere
Caslon Way
Danescroft
Middlefields
Lindencroft
Eastern Way
Farm Close
Croft Lane
Cashio Lane
Church Lane
Norton St Nicholas Primary School
Southfields
Sherwood
Woodhurst
Grange Road
Lammas Way
Stonnells Close
Westholme
Wilbury Road
Eastholm
Eastholm Green
Norton School
Norton Way North
Common View
North Avenue
Green Lane
Talbot Way
Cade Close
Sandy Way
Kristiansand Way
Flint Road
Works
Blackhorse Road
Knap Close
Works Road
Winton Close
Cromwell Green
Cromwell Road
Glebe Road
Pyms Close
Hampden Close
Tabbs Close
Pascal Way
Norton Common
Letchworth Swimming Pool
Oakfield
Icknield Way Path
Icknield Way
The Arches
Iceni Court
Ascot Industrial Estate
Shaftesbury Industrial Centre
Green Lane Industrial Estate
Saunders Close
Diamond Industrial Centre
Jubilee Trading Estate
Jubilee Road
Lacre Way
Hadrian Way
Cotton Brown Park
Works Road
The Coppens
Groveland Way
Littlebury Cl
PO
P
7
14
19
E F G H
1 2 3 4 5
22 23

14
8
20
13
A
B
C
D
1
2
3
4
5
524
25
36
35
234
adwell
Lane
A1(M)
A507
River Ivel
Norton
Mill Lane
Icknield Way Path
Blackhorse Farm
NORTH ROAD
Norton Road
Salisbury Road
Bygrave Road
Marquis Business Centre
Ashville Trading Estate
Larkins Cl
Baldock Station
STATION RD
Icknield Way
Works
Football Cl
Orch Road
Church Street
Pond Lane
The Sycamores
Cemetery
Coachman's Lane
Norton Crescent
West Avenue
Pepys Way
Hopewell Road
HITCHIN ST
WHITEHORSE STREET
HIGH STREET
CLOTHALL ROAD
California
Grosvenor Road
Hartsfield Primary School
Yeomanry Drive
Sale Drive
Stane St
Hurst Close
Bush
Wynn Close
Mercia Road
Baldock
Wallington Rd
Simpson Drive
Thurnall Close
Park Street
Knights Templar School
LETCHWORTH ROAD
Weston Way
Works Road
Flint Road
Knap Close
Winton Close
Blackhorse Road
Hadrian Way
Diamond Industrial Centre
Jubilee Trading Estate
Cotton Brown Park
Lacre Way
Brandles School
Mansfield Road
Holroyd Crescent
Baldock Health Ce
A6141
The Tene
The Orch
Pinnocks Lane
Pembroke Road
Roman Lane
South Road
Walnut Avenue
Limekiln La
Penfold Cl
St Johns RC Primary
Baldock Industrial Estate
Chilvers Bank
The Row
Alder Close
Half Farm
PO
1 grid square represents 500 metres

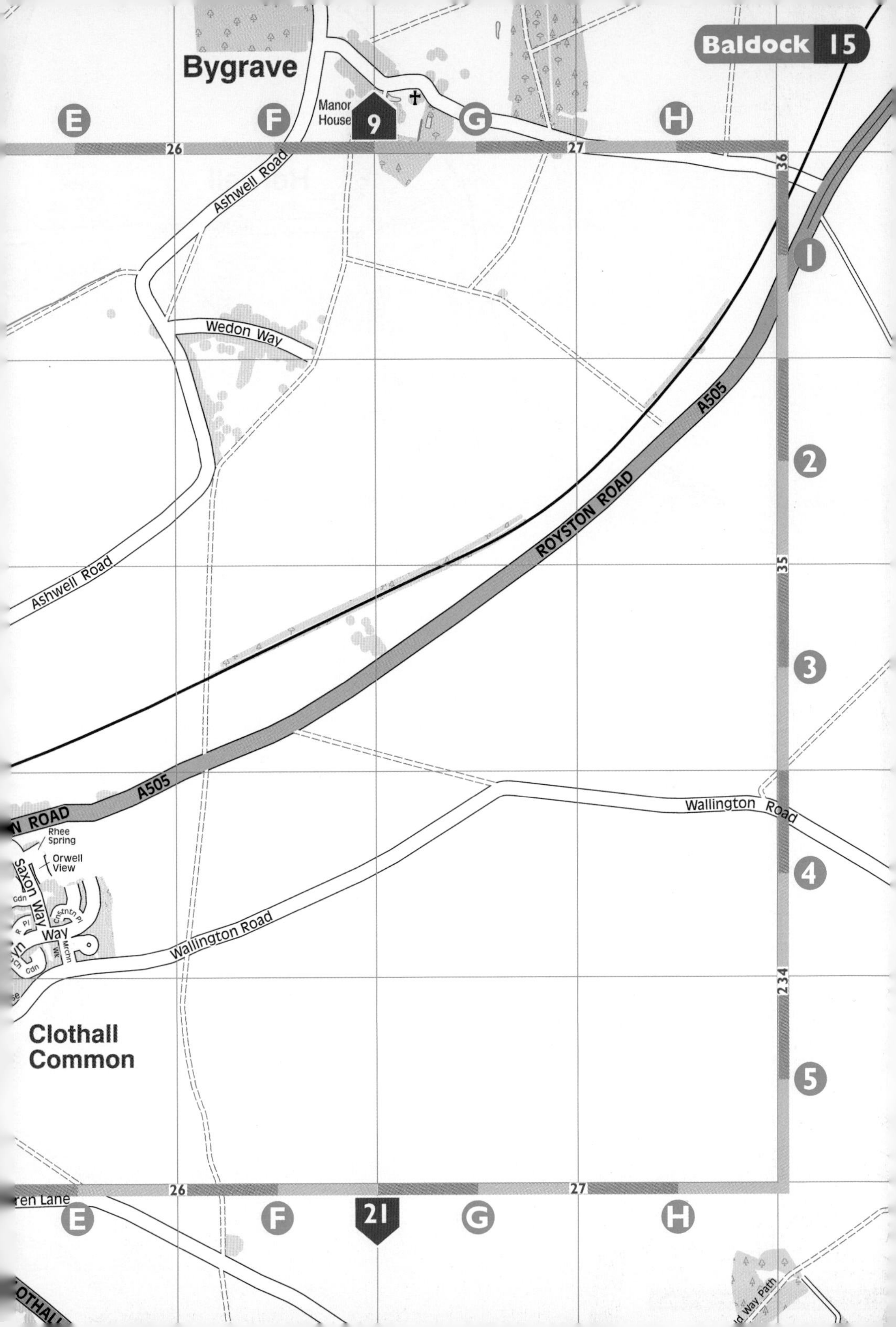
Bygrave
Manor House
9
E
F
G
H
26
27
36
35
234
1
2
3
4
5
Ashwell Road
Wedon Way
ROYSTON ROAD
A505
Wallington Road
Rhee Spring
Orwell View
Saxon Way
Clothall Common
ren Lane
21
Way Path

A
B
10
C
D
516
17
Holwell
Gurney's Lane
Meadow Farm
Holwell Road
Rand's Meadow
Ashc
Farm
Pirton Road
Lordship Farm
hire County
hire County
Waterloo Lane
Holwell Road
New Wrights Farm
1
2
3
4
5
33
32
231
P
Fa
Icknield Way Path
Icknield Way Path
Icknield Way Pa
Westmill Lane
Westmill Lane
516
17
A
B
22
C
D
1 grid square represents 500 metres

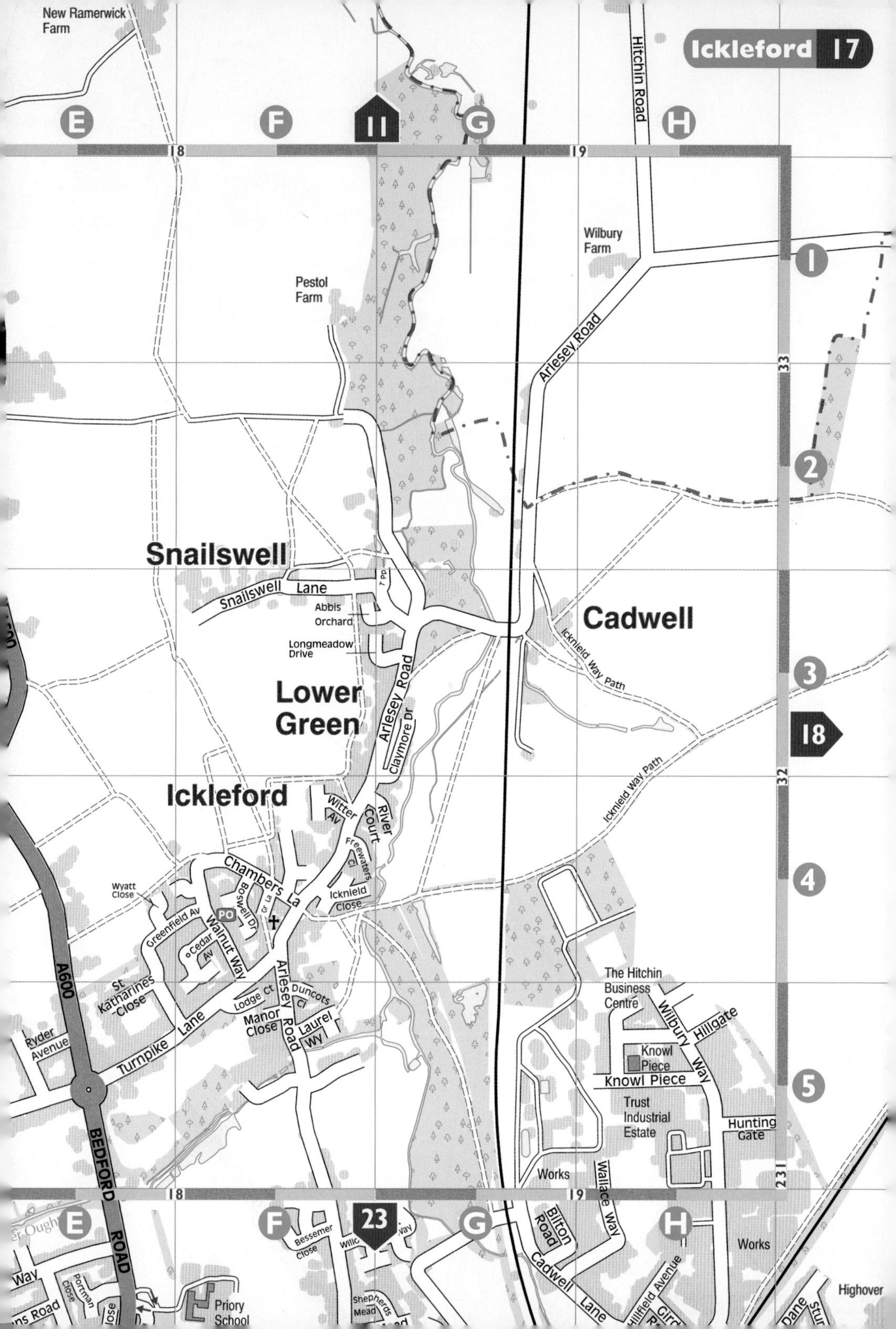
New Ramerwick Farm
E
F
11
G
H
18
19
Hitchin Road
Wilbury Farm
1
Pestol Farm
Arlesey Road
33
2
Snailswell
Snailswell Lane
T Pd
Abbis Orchard
Longmeadow Drive
Cadwell
Icknield Way Path
Lower Green
Arlesey Road
Claymore Dr
3
18
32
Ickleford
Witter Av
River Court
Freewaters Cl
Icknield Way Path
Chambers La
Boswell Dr
Gr La
Icknield Close
4
Wyatt Close
Greenfield Av
PO
Walnut Way
Cedar Av
A600
St Katharines Close
Lodge Ct
Duncots Cl
Arlesey Road
Manor Close
Laurel Wy
The Hitchin Business Centre
Wilbury Way
Hillgate
Knowl Piece
Knowl Piece
Ryder Avenue
Turnpike Lane
5
Trust Industrial Estate
Hunting Gate
BEDFORD ROAD
Works
Wallace Way
231
18
19
E
F
23
G
H
Bessemer Close
Bilton Road
Works
Way
Portman Close
Cadwell Lane
Hillfield Avenue
Shepherds Mead
Highover
Priory School

Standalone Farm Centre
A
B
C
D
12
24
17
5 20
21
33
32
231
1
2
3
4
5
LETCHWORTH
Wilbury Road
Furlay Close
David Evans Ct
Beech Hill
Chasten Hill
Valley Road
Warren Close
Fullers Court
Haymoor
Longmead
Cowslip
Arlesey New Road
Stotfold Road
Wilbury Hills Road
Wilbury Close
Eldefield
Runnalow
Bedford Road
Wilbury Junior School
Redhoods Way East
Rowan Crescent
Wilburyhill Farm
Romany Close
Mullway
Hall Mead
Monklands
Bursland
Archers
Haselfoot
Redhoods Way West
Icknield Green
Saffron Hill
Marmet Av
Abbotts Road
Icknield Infant School
Way
Cemetery
Monks Close
Icknield Way
Chagny Close
Station
Horace Gay Gdns
The Dale
Broadwater Dale
Campfield Way
Highover Road
Martin Way
Works
Burnell Rise
Burnell Walk
Campers Walk
Campers Road
Springshott
Westbury Place
Spring
Fearnhill Sports Centre
Fearnhill School
Campers Avenue
Chiltern View
High
Hillbrow
West View
Avenue
Unwin Close
Parker Close
Road
St Thomas More RC Primary School
Oak Tree Cl
Sollershott West
Highfield
Highfield School
North Hertfordshire Secondary Centre
Briar Patch Lane
HITCHIN ROAD
A505
Pasture Road
Wilbury Way
Hillgate
Hunting Gate
Works
Highover Farm
Collison Close
Close
Roundwood
Crovelands Avenue
CAMBRIDGE RD
Golf Course
Kite Way
Jay Close
Linnet Close
The Bird

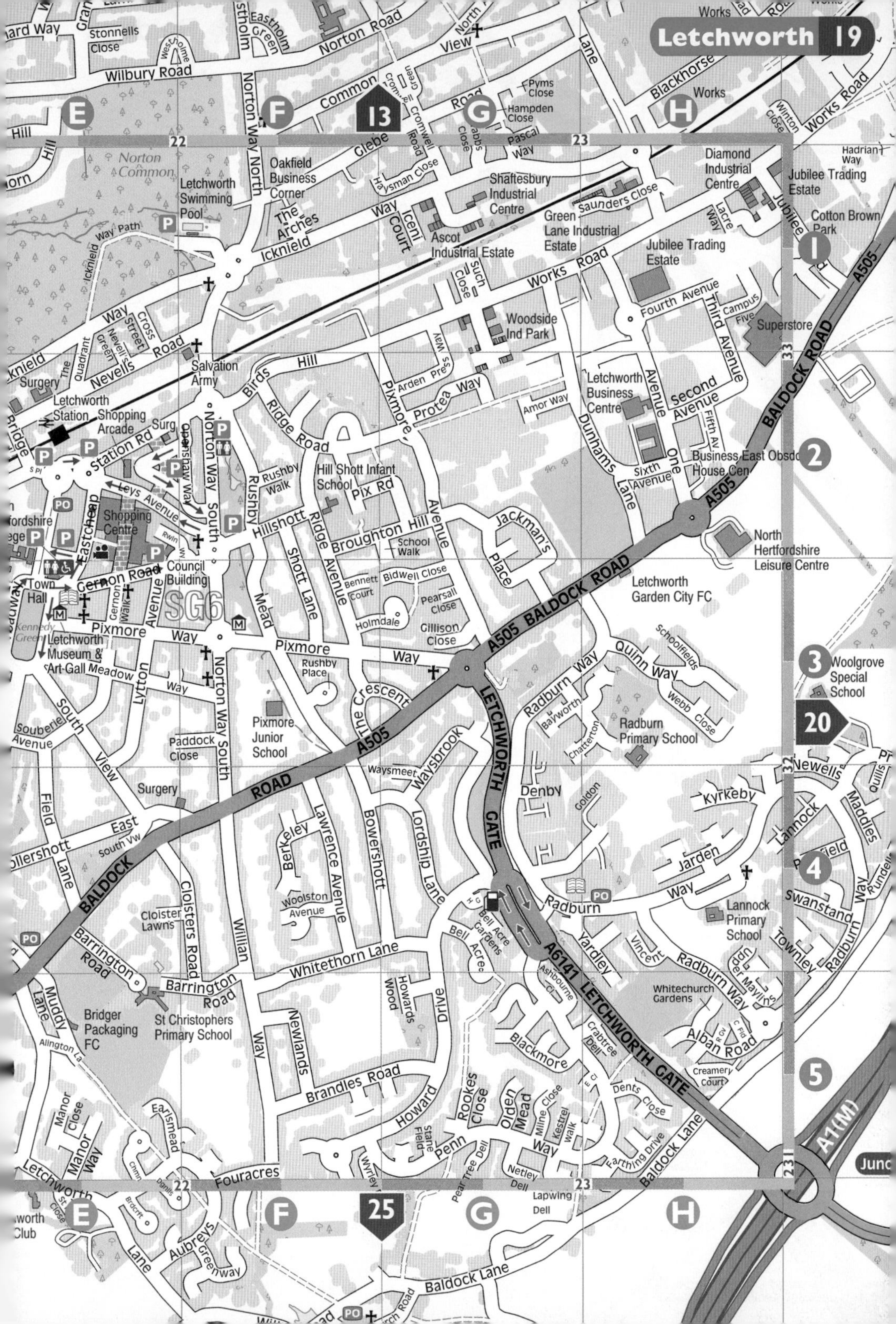
Letchworth
19
13
20
25
E
F
G
H
22
23
1
2
3
4
5
32
33
231
Norton Road
Wilbury Road
Stonnells Close
Westholme
Eastholm Green
Norton Way North
Common View
North
Cromwell Green
Cromwell Road
Pyms Close
Hampden Close
Pascal Way
Glebe Road
Blackhorse Road
Works Road
Winton Close
Works
Norton Common
Letchworth Swimming Pool
Oakfield Business Corner
The Arches
Icknield Way
Icknield Way Path
Haysman Close
Iceni Court
Shaftesbury Industrial Centre
Ascot Industrial Estate
Green Lane Industrial Estate
Saunders Close
Diamond Industrial Centre
Jubilee Trading Estate
Hadrian Way
Lacre Way
Jubilee Road
Cotton Brown Park
Such Close
Woodside Ind Park
Fourth Avenue
Third Avenue
Campus Five
Superstore
Arden Press Way
Protea Way
Amor Way
Letchworth Business Centre
Second Avenue
Fifth Av
Sixth Avenue
One Avenue
Dunhams Lane
Business East
House
A505
BALDOCK ROAD
A505 BALDOCK ROAD
North Hertfordshire Leisure Centre
Letchworth Garden City FC
Cross Street
Nevells Green
The Quadrant
Nevells Road
Salvation Army
Surgery
Letchworth Station
Shopping Arcade
Station Rd
Surg
Openshaw Way
Norton Way South
Birds Hill
Ridge Road
Pixmore Avenue
Hill Shott Infant School
Pix Rd
Rushby Walk
Rushby Mead
Hillshott
Leys Avenue
Eastcheap
Shopping Centre
Gernon Road
Council Building
SG6
Town Hall
Gernon Walk
Broughton Hill
School Walk
Ridge Avenue
Shott Lane
Bennett Court
Bidwell Close
Pearsall Close
Holmdale
Gillison Close
Jackman's Place
Schoolfields
Quinn Way
Radburn Way
Bayworth
Chatterton
Radburn Primary School
Webb Close
Woolgrove Special School
Kennedy Gardens
Letchworth Museum & Art Gall
Pixmore Way
Meadow Way
Lytton Avenue
South View
Souberie Avenue
Rushby Place
The Crescent
Pixmore Junior School
Paddock Close
LETCHWORTH GATE
Waysbrook
Waysmeet
Denby
Goldon
Newells
Kyrkeby
Lannock
Maddles
Quills
Pix Field
Rundells
Jarden
Field Lane
East View
South Vw
Hollershott
Surgery
ROAD
BALDOCK
Berkeley
Lawrence Avenue
Bowershott
Lordship Lane
Woolston Avenue
Cloisters Road
Cloister Lawns
Willian Way
Radburn Way
Swanstand
Townley
Radburn Way
Lannock Primary School
Yardley
Vincent
Bell Acre Gardens
Bell Acre
Whitethorn Lane
A6141 LETCHWORTH GATE
Ashbourne Cl
Whitechurch Gardens
Under Mayling
Barrington Road
Muddy Lane
Bridger Packaging FC
St Christophers Primary School
Allington La
Howards Wood
Drive
Newlands
Blackmore
Crabtree Dell
Alban Road
Creamery Court
Dents Close
Brandles Road
Howard Drive
Rookes Close
Olden Mead
Milne Close
Kestrel Walk
Manor Close
Manor Way
Earlsmead
Stane Field
Penn Way
Farthing Drive
Baldock Lane
A1(M)
Junc
Letchworth
Fouracres
Wyrley
Pear Tree Dell
Netley Dell
Lapwing Dell
Club
Lane
Aubreys
Greenway
Baldock Lane
PO
P

20
14
19
26
Baldock
A
B
C
D
1
2
3
4
5
524
25
33
32
231
Works
Works Road
Knap Close
Winton Close
West Avenue
Pepys Way
Hopewell Road
Hitchin Road
Letchworth Road
Park Street
Knights Templar School
High Street
Simpson Drive
The Tene
The Orchard
Pinnocks Lane
Pembroke Road
Roman Lane
Wallington Road
Clothall Road
A1(M)
Hadrian Way
Diamond Industrial Centre
Jubilee Trading Estate
Lacre Way
Jubilee Road
Cotton Brown Park
Jubilee Trading Estate
Brandles School
Weston Way
Mansfield Road
Park Drive
Park Close
Holroyd Crescent
Baldock Health Cen
A6141
South Road
Walnut Avenue
Laxton Gardens
Limekiln La
Penfold Cl
St Johns RC Primary School
Baldock Industrial Estate
Turpin's Way
Anchor Road
Hillcrest
Pryor Road
Byrd Walk
Ivel Way
Icknield Way
Chilvers Bank
The Glade
The Close
The Leas
Hill Top
The Rise
PO
St Mary's Way
The Rowans
Alder Close
The Spinney
Bondor Business Cen
Elmwd Av
Nightingale Way
Mons Avenue
London Road
Page Close
Woodland Way
Woodland Wy
St Marys Junior & Infant School
The Dell
Wll Wy
Third Avenue
Campus Five
Superstore
Baldock Road
A505
Second Avenue
Fifth Av
Business House Cen
Obsdoc
North Hertfordshire Leisure Centre
Baldock Lane
Ashton's Lane
Chiltern Road
Chalk Hills
Beechwood Close
Hatch Lane
Woolgrove Special School
Webb Close
Newells
Pryor Way
Kyrkeby
Quills
Maddles
Oakhill
Lannock
Parkfield
Jarden
Rundells
Swanstand
Radburn Way
Townley
Lannock Primary School
Radburn Way
Upper Mayline
Alban Road
Creamery Court
Junction 9
B197
1 grid square represents 500 metres

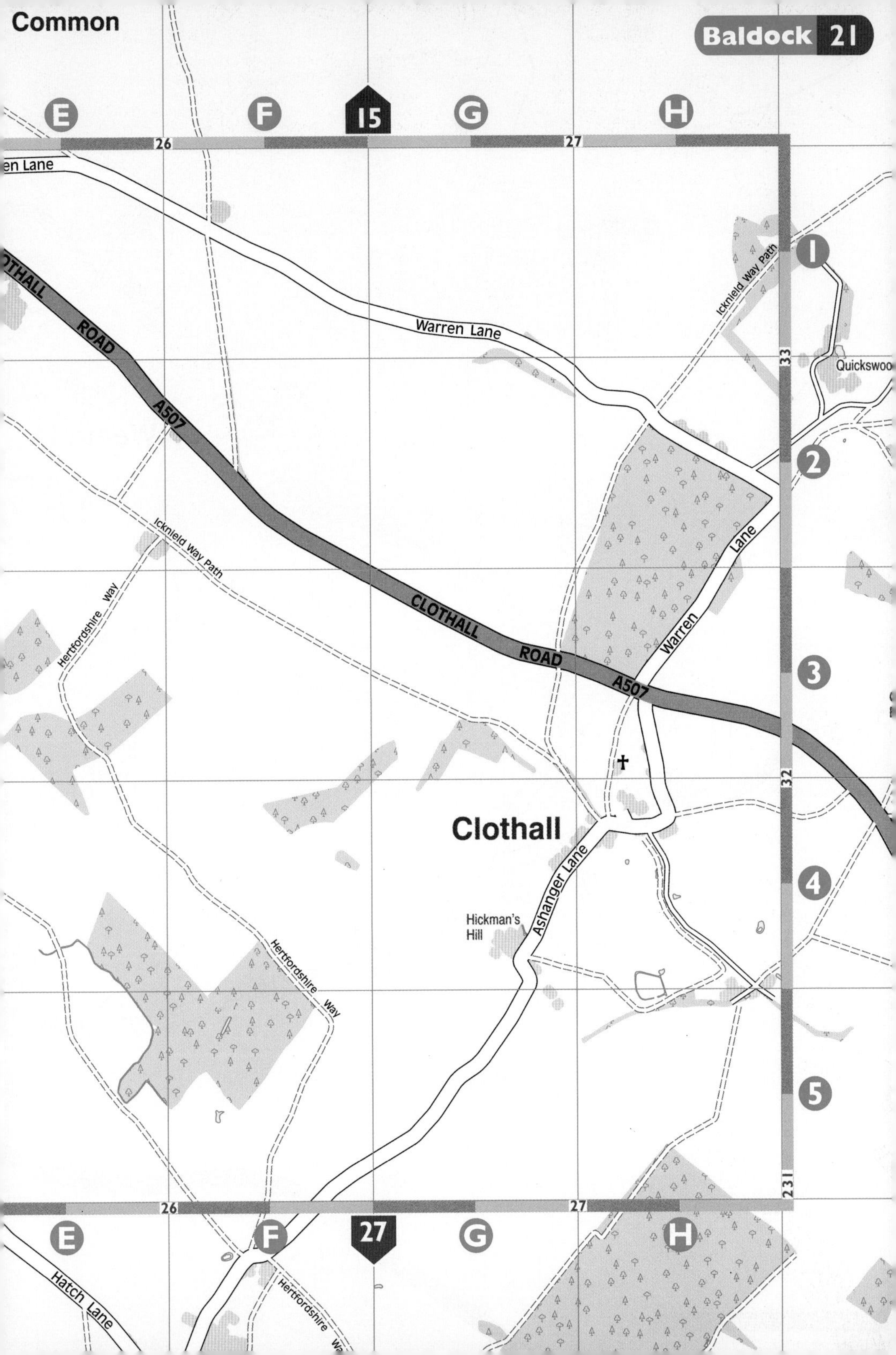
E
F
15
G
H
26
27
en Lane
Warren Lane
CLOTHALL ROAD
A507
Icknield Way Path
Quickswoo
33
1
2
3
4
5
Icknield Way Path
Hertfordshire Way
Warren Lane
CLOTHALL ROAD
A507
32
Clothall
Ashanger Lane
Hickman's Hill
Hertfordshire Way
231
26
27
E
F
27
G
H
Hatch Lane
Hertfordshire Wa

Icknield Way Path
Path
A
B
16
C
D
516
17
31
30
229
1
2
3
4
5
Westmill Lane
Westmill Lane
Swinburne Av
Hine Way
Close
Westmill
Bingen Road
Moss Way
Oughtonhead Common Nature Reserve
Oughtonhead Lane
Oughton Head Farm
Hitchin Road
ROAD
B655
Pirton Cross
Carters Lane (Wibbly Wobbley Lane)
Manley Hwy
PIRTON
ROAD
Foxholes
Offley Bottom
Offley Cross
1 grid square represents 500 metres

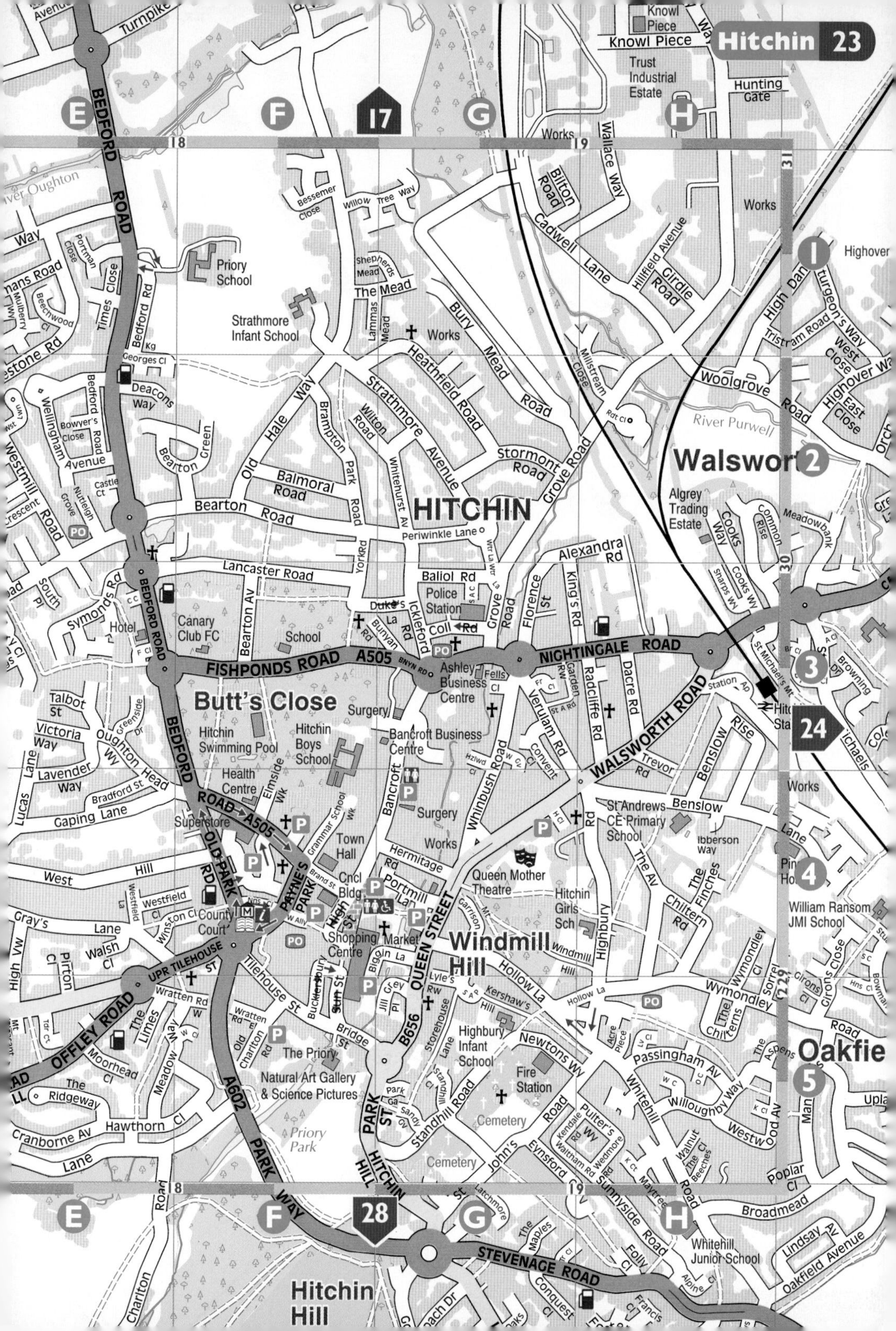

HITCHIN
Walsworth
Windmill Hill
Butt's Close
Hitchin Hill
Oakfield
BEDFORD ROAD
FISHPONDS ROAD A505
NIGHTINGALE ROAD
WALSWORTH ROAD
QUEEN STREET
B656
OFFLEY ROAD
UPR TILEHOUSE ST
PARK WAY
A602
STEVENAGE ROAD
HITCHIN HILL
PARK ST
PAYNE'S PARK
OLD PARK RD
Turnpike Lane
Knowl Piece
Trust Industrial Estate
Hunting Gate
Works
Wallace Way
Bilton Road
Cadwell Lane
Hillfield Avenue
Girdle Road
Bessemer Close
Willow Tree Way
Priory School
Portman Close
Times Close
Bedford Rd
Beechwood Cl
Strathmore Infant School
Shepherds Mead
The Mead
Lammas Mead
Bury Mead Road
Heathfield Road
Strathmore Avenue
Millstream Close
Woolgrove Road
River Purwell
Tristram Road
Sturgeon's Way
West Close
East Close
Highover Way
High Dane
Georges Cl
Deacons Way
Wellingham Avenue
Bowyer's Close
Bedford Road
Bearton Green
Old Hale Way
Brampton Park Road
Wilton Road
Whitehurst Av
Stormont Road
Grove Road
Balmoral Road
Bearton Road
Westmill Road
Castle Ct
Nuttleigh Grove
Periwinkle Lane
Algrey Trading Estate
Cooks Way
Common Rise
Meadowbank
Alexandra Rd
Lancaster Road
York Rd
Baliol Rd
Police Station
Duke's La
Bunyan Rd
Icklesford Rd
Coll Rd
Florence St
King's Rd
Symonds Rd
Hotel
Canary Club FC
Bearton Av
School
Ashley Business Centre
Fells Cl
Verulam Rd
Garden Rw
Radcliffe Rd
Dacre Rd
Station Ap
St Michael's Mt
Hitchin Station
Talbot St
Victoria Way
Oughton Head Wy
Lavender Way
Lucas Lane
Hitchin Swimming Pool
Hitchin Boys School
Surgery
Bancroft Business Centre
Whinbush Road
Convent Cl
Trevor Rd
Benslow Rise
Bradford St
Gaping Lane
Health Centre
Elmside Wk
Grammar School Wk
Bancroft
Works
St Andrews CE Primary School
Benslow Lane
Ibberson Way
Superstore
West Hill
Town Hall
Hermitage Rd
Queen Mother Theatre
The Av
The Finches
Westfield La
Westfield Cl
Winston Cl
County Court
Cncl Bldg
Portmill La
Carrison Mt
Hitchin Girls Sch
Highbury
Chiltern Rd
William Ransom JMI School
Gray's Lane
Walsh Cl
High St
Shopping Centre
Market
Windmill Hill
Wymondley Cl
Sorrel Garth
Girons Close
Pirton Cl
High Vw
Wratten Rd W
Tilehouse St
Bucklersbury
Sun St
Biggin La
Lyle's Rw
Jill Grey Pl
Kershaw's Hill
Hollow La
Wymondley Road
The Chilterns
The Limes
Meadow Way
Wratten Rd E
Old Charlton Rd
The Priory
Bridge St
Storehouse Lane
Highbury Infant School
Newtons Wy
Acre Piece
Passingham Av
Willoughby Way
The Aspens
Moorhead Cl
The Ridgeway
Natural Art Gallery & Science Pictures
Standhill Cl
Standhill Road
Fire Station
Cemetery
Pulter's Wy
Whitehill Road
Westwood Av
Manor Cres
Hawthorn Cl
Cranborne Av
Lane
Priory Park
Sandy Gv
John's Road
Eynsford Rd
Waltham Rd
Wedmore Rd
Walnut
The Cl
Beeches
Poplar Cl
Charlton Road
Latchmore
The Maples
Sunnyside Road
Maytree
Folly Cl
Broadmead
Whitehill Junior School
Lindsay Av
Oakfield Avenue
Conquest Cl
Alpine Cl
Francis
E
F
G
H
17
18
19
24
28
29
30
31
1
2
3
4
5

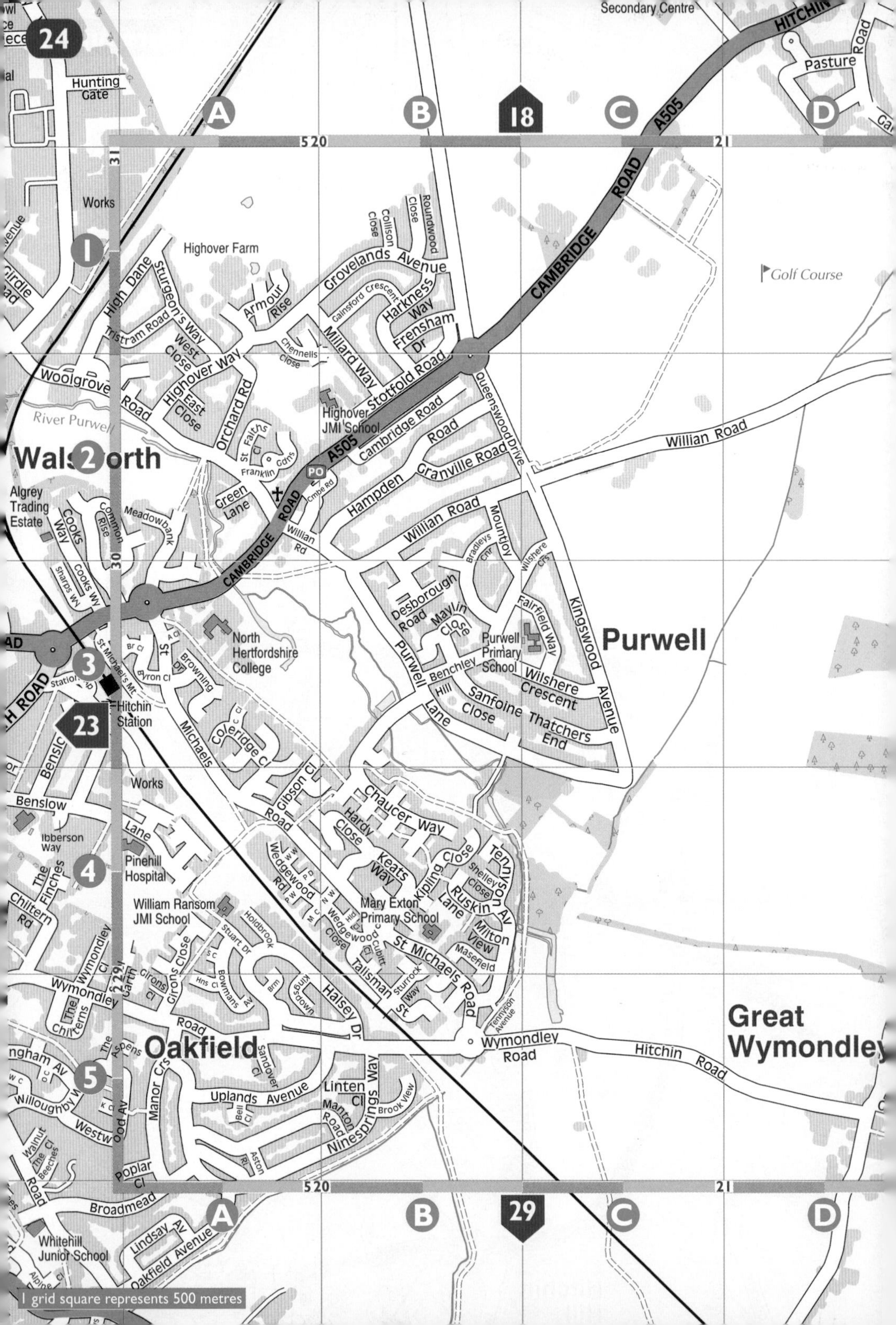
24
Hunting Gate
Works
Highover Farm
Walsworth
Algrey Trading Estate
River Purwell
Woolgrove Road
High Dane
Sturgeon's Way
Tristram Road
West Close
East Close
Highover Way
Orchard Rd
Armour Rise
Chennells Close
Grovelands Avenue
Gainsford Crescent
Collison Close
Roundwood Close
Harkness Way
Frensham Dr
Millard Way
Stotfold Road
Highover JMI School
Cambridge Road
CAMBRIDGE ROAD
A505
St Faiths Cl
Franklin Gdns
PO
Cmbe Rd
Green Lane
Meadowbank
Common Rise
Cooks Way
Sharps Wy
Cooks Wy
William Rd
Hampden Road
Granville Road
Queenswood Drive
Willian Road
Mountjoy
Bradleys Cnr
Wilshere Crs
Desborough Road
Maylin Close
Fairfield Way
Kingswood Avenue
Purwell
Purwell Primary School
Wilshere Crescent
Benchley Hill
Purwell Lane
Sanfoine Close
Thatchers End
North Hertfordshire College
St Michaels Mt
Browning Dr
Byron Cl
Hitchin Station
Station Ap
23
Coleridge Cl
St Michaels Road
Gibson Cl
Chaucer Way
Hardy Close
Keats Way
Kipling Close
Tennyson Av
Shelley Close
Ruskin Lane
Milton View
Masefield
Wedgewood Rd
Wedgewood Close
Mary Exton Primary School
St Michaels Road
Talisman St
Sturrock Way
Cubitt Cl
Works
Benslow
Benslow Lane
Ibberson Way
Pinehill Hospital
The Finches
Chiltern Rd
William Ransom JMI School
Holdbrook
Stuart Dr
Bowmans Av
Kingsdown
Halsey Dr
Girons Close
Girons Cl
Garth
Wymondley Cl
Wymondley Road
The Chilterns
Oakfield
Sandover Cl
Tennyson Avenue
Wymondley Road
Hitchin Road
Great Wymondley
Manor Crs
Uplands Avenue
Linten Cl
Ninesprings Way
Brook View
Manton Road
Bell Cl
Aston
Willoughby Wy
Westwood Av
The Aspens
Walnut
The Cl
Beeches
Road
Poplar Cl
Broadmead
Lindsay Av
Oakfield Avenue
Whitehill Junior School
Golf Course
Pasture Road
Secondary Centre
HITCHIN
A B C D
18
29
520
21
31
30
29
1 2 3 4 5
1 grid square represents 500 metres

Willian
Willian Road
Baldock Lane
Willian Church Road
Wymondley Road
Letchworth Lane
Fouracres
Aubreys
Greenway
Brandles Road
Howard
Rookes Close
Olden Mead
Milne Close
Kestrel Walk
Penn Way
Stane Field
Pear Tree
Netley Dell
Lapwing Dell
Dents Close
Farthing Drive
Blackmore
Manor Close
Earlsmead
Roxley Court
Hertfordshire Way
Jack's Hill
A1(M)
B197
Graveley Lane
NORTH GATE
19
26
30
22
23
E
F
G
H
1
2
3
4
5

26
A1(M)
Junction 9
A6141
B197
Lannock Hill
Lannock Manor Farm
Jack's Hill
Chesfield Downs Golf Club
Golf Course
How Wood
Hertfordshire Way
20
25
31
A
B
C
D
1
2
3
4
5
524
25
231
230
229
1 grid square represents 500 metres

E
F
21
G
H
26
27
31
30
29
Hatch Lane
Hertfordshire Way
Green End
Mill Lane
Fore Street
Weston
Weston Bury
Street
Maiden
Munts Meadow
School La
Works
Weston Primary School
Church End
Church Lane
Hitchin Road
Friars Road
PO
Manor Ho
Marlborough Cl
Woodlands Meade
Damask Green
Damask Close
Rowan Cl
amask
reen
Road
Hertfordshire Way
Weston Park
Hertfordshire Way
Warren's Green
Weston Lodge
Hall's Green
PH
Fai
Far
1
2
3
4
5
32
Hertfordshire Way
ne End Lane
Warrensgreen La
Tilekiln Farm

MOORHEAD HILL
Moorhead Cl
The Ridgeway
Cranborne Av
Hawthorn Cl
Willow Lane
Meadow
The Priory
Natural Art Gallery & Science Pictures
Priory Park
A602 PARK WAY
PARK ST
HITCHIN HILL
Infant School
Fire Station
Cemetery
Standhill Road
St John's Road
Eynsford Ct
Pulter's Wy
Passingham Av
Whitehill
Willoughby Way
Sunnyside Road
Maytrees
The Beeches
Whitehill Junior School
STEVENAGE ROAD
Latchmore Cl
The Maples
Folly Cl
Conquest Cl
Francis Cl
Alpine Cl
Foster Dr
Coach Dr
Hitchin Hill
Charlton Road
Charlton
Brick Kiln Lane
Gosmore Road
Lister Av
Oaks Cl
LONDON ROAD
Matthew Ga
Blackhorse Lane
Mowbray Gdns
Dale Cl
Bramshott Close
Grange Cl
Langbridge
Sycamore Cl
Priory Wy
Newlands Lane
Rowan Gv
B656
Broadmeadow
Ride Av
Larch
Ash Dr
Tall Trees
Millfield La
Maydencroft Lane
Wellhead
Maydencroft Manor
Hitchin Road
Gosmore Ley Cl
Mill Lane
Gosmore
Mill Road
Orchard Cl
High St
The Crs
Waterdell Lane
PO
Preston Road
Thistley Lane
St Ibb
Tatmore Place
518
19
28
27
226
A
B
C
D
1
2
3
4
5
23
1 grid square represents 500 metres

Oakfield
Wymondley Road
Hitchin Road
Wymondley
Manor Crs
Sandover Cl
Uplands Avenue
Bell Cl
Linten Cl
Manton Road
Ninesprings Way
Brook View
Aston
Graveley Road
24
20
21
E
F
G
H
Hertfordshire Way
Lindsay Av
Oakfield Avenue
I
A602
Kingshott School
28
Arch Road
Priory Lane
Ashbrook
A602
Wymondley Primary School
Grimstone Road
Little Wymondley
2
Stevenage Road
Ashbrook Lane
Siccut Road
Priory View
Works
Elms Close
Bladon Cl
Tower Cl
Church Path
Blakemore End Road
3
30
St Ippolyts Primary School
East View
Wym
Bury
27
Cemetery
Stevenage Road
Ippollitts
Titmore Green
4
Redcoats
Sperberry Hill
B656
5
oe
226
20
21
E
F
G
H
LONDON ROAD
ire Way

30
25
29
34
A
B
C
D
1
2
3
4
5
Graveley Road
Graveley Lane
Hertfordshire Way
Priory Lane
Priory View
Elms Close
Bladon Cl
Tower Cl
Church Path
Wymondley Bury
A602
Chantry Lane
Old Chantry Lane
Todd's Green
Stevenage Road
A1(M)
Junction 8
B197
GRAVELEY ROAD
A602 HITCHIN ROAD
HIGH STREET
Graveley Primary School
Ashwell Common La
Ashwell Close
Turf
Oak Lane
Pondside
Milksey Lane
Grinders End
Church
Superstore
Lister Hospital
A&E
Lister Close
Stevenage Business Park
Coreys Mill Lane
Baron Ct
Ingleside
Hernes Road
Chapman Road
Drive
The Old Walled Garden
Higgins Walk
Whitney Drive
John Henry Newman RC School
NORTH ROAD
Daltry Road
Daltry Close
Woodfield Road
Tudor Close
Burymead
Caister Close
Kessingland Av
Gorleston Cl
Aldeburgh Close
Fishers Green
Sheringham Avenue
Mundesley Close
Bawdsey Close
Skegness Road
Berwick Close
Southsea Road
Lymington Road
Jubilee Road
Fisher's Green Road
A1072
Essex Road
Franklin's Rd
1 grid square represents 500 metres

E
F
26
G
H
24
25
I
Manor Farm
Hertfordshire Way
Surgery
Chesfield Park
Hertfordshire Way
Hertfordshire Way
2
28
Riccat La
Weston Road
Great Ashby Way
Weston Rd
Wansbeck Cl
Cherwell Dr
Tamar Cl
3
32
St Davids Cl
Manchester
Old Bourne Way
St Andrews Drive
Nwcstl Cl
Weston Road
Way
Leys Primary School
Salisbury Road
Winchester Close
Lincoln Road
27
Ripon Road
Beverley Road
4
Surgery
St Nicholas Health Cen
Iona Close
Islington
Canterbury Way
Rook's Nest
Lancaster Cl
Guildford Close
St Nicholas
Pilgrims Way
Exeter Close
Southwark Close
Thurlow Close
Arnold Close
Road
Morgan Cl
Wilson Close
Mathews Close
St Al Ln
Weston Road
St Albans Drive
Durham Rd
Chester Road
Coventry Close
Norwich Close
Close
York Road
The Giles Infant & Junior School
Cemetery
The Bury
Lane
Road
5
Martins Wood Primary School
Brambles
Nicholas Place
Chestnut Walk
Bader Close
Trotts Hill Primary School
Jessop Road
Jessop Road
Bradman Wy
VERITY WAY
A1072
Trafford Close
Trent Close
Wisden Road
PO
226
Mildmay
24
25
E
F
35
G
H
Almond Hill School
Grace Way
Wisden Road
Derby Way
A1155
Barclay School
Weston Road
Almonds
Cemetery
Providence Grove
Vardon Road
Sutcliffe Close
Pin Green

Warren's Green
Hall's Green
Hertfordshire Way
A B C D
27
526
1 2 3 4 5
28
Tilekiln Farm
Dane End Lane
Warrensgreen Lane
Dane End
Ashby Way
Blackdown Cl
Fairfield Wy
Grasmere
Lomond Way
Gt Ashby Wy
Neagh Cl
Lowes Cl
Serpentine Close
Great Ashby Way
Windermere Cl
Thirlmere
Ullswater Cl
Boxbury Farm
Box Wood
31
St Nicholas Recreation Centre
Leys Primary School
Salisbury Road
Lincoln Road
Winchester Close
Whitworth Road
Senate Place
Wedgwood Court
Boulton Road
Wedgwood Way
Wedgewood Park
Wedgewood Gate Industrial Estate
Beverley Road
Pilgrims Way
Exeter Close
Wedgwood Gate
Stevenage Business Park
Pin Green Industrial Est
Cartwright Road
Southwark Close
Ely Close
Works
Coventry Close
Chester Road
Norwich Close
Martins Way
Ascot Crescent
Sefton Road
Bradman Wy
Jessop Road
VERITY WAY
Martins Wood Primary School
Gordian Way
Gresley Way
Trajan Gate
Lingfield Road
Mildmay Road
Sandown Road
Julia Gate
Valerian Way
Neptune
PO
36
Derby Way
Round Diamond Primary School
Chepstow Close
Wetherby Close
Doncaster
Ayr Close
Pacatian Way
Tacitus Cl
Alexander Gate
Emperors Ga
Fortuna Cl
Pin Green
A1155
FAIRLANDS WAY
B1037
The Pastures
1 grid square represents 500 metres

E
F
G
H
28
29
Works
I
Cro
Howells Farm
2
B1037
3
Churchend Common
WHITE HILL
27
4
Beecroft Lane
Manor Farm
Church End
Kitcheners Lane
B1037
PH
Bockings
Winters Lane
Walkern
Brockwell Shott
HIGH ST
Totts Lane
Froghall Lane
PO
5
Aubries
Cherry Tree Rise
Moors Ley
226
STEVENAGE ROAD
37
Finches End
Street
The Maltings
Wrights Meadow

34
30
33
38
A
B
C
D
1
2
3
4
5
522
23
26
25
224
Fishers Green
Symonds Green
Norton Green
A1(M)
A1072
A1155
GUNNELS WOOD ROAD
FAIRLANDS WAY
LYTTON WAY
John Henry Newman RC School
The Symonds Green Health Centre
Woolenwick Junior & Infant School
Hyatt Trading Estate
Business & Technology Centre
Bowmans Trading Estate
Industrial Area
Hollywood Bowl
Stevenage Leisure Park
Stevenage Station
Surgery
Works
Hotel
Factory
Brighton Way
Berwick Close
Hastings Close
Shoreham Close
Clovelly Way
Hopton Road
Skegness Road
Minehead Way
Symonds Green Road
Yarmouth Road
Filey Close
Blyth Close
Scarborough Avenue
Blakeney Road
Symonds Green Lane
Eastbourne Av
Bude Crs
Newlyn Close
Redcar Drive
Rutherford Close
Meadway
Crompton Road
Cavendish Road
Babbage Road
Corton Close
Fisher's Green Road
Jubilee Road
Lymington Road
Huntingdon Road
Southsea Road
Mundesley Close
Bawdsey Close
Kessingland Av
Aldeburgh Close
Chapman Road
Drive
Prestatyn Cl
Colwyn Close
Fairview Road
Fleetwood Crs
Morecambe Cl
Brixham Close
Torquay Crs
Mayles Cl
Hilton Close
Julian's Road
Julian's Court
Essex Road
Orchard Rd
Orchard Crescent
Bridge Rd W
Angotts Mdw
Larkinson
Ivel Road
Green St
Woolners Way
Brickkiln Road
Chequers Bridge Road
Primett Road
Maxwell Road
Mozart Court
Argyle Way
Fulton Close
Gordon
Kings Way
Bessemer Drive
Caxton Way
Potters Lane
Chadwell Road
Six Hills Way
Shepherds Lane
Kitching Lane
Dyes Lane
Higgins Walk
Whitney Dr
Tudor Close
Burymead
Franklin's Rd
Dewpond Close
James Way
Bwl Gn
High St
Basils Road
Bell La
Mid Rw
R Yd
Drapers Wy
PO
P
1 grid square represents 500 metres

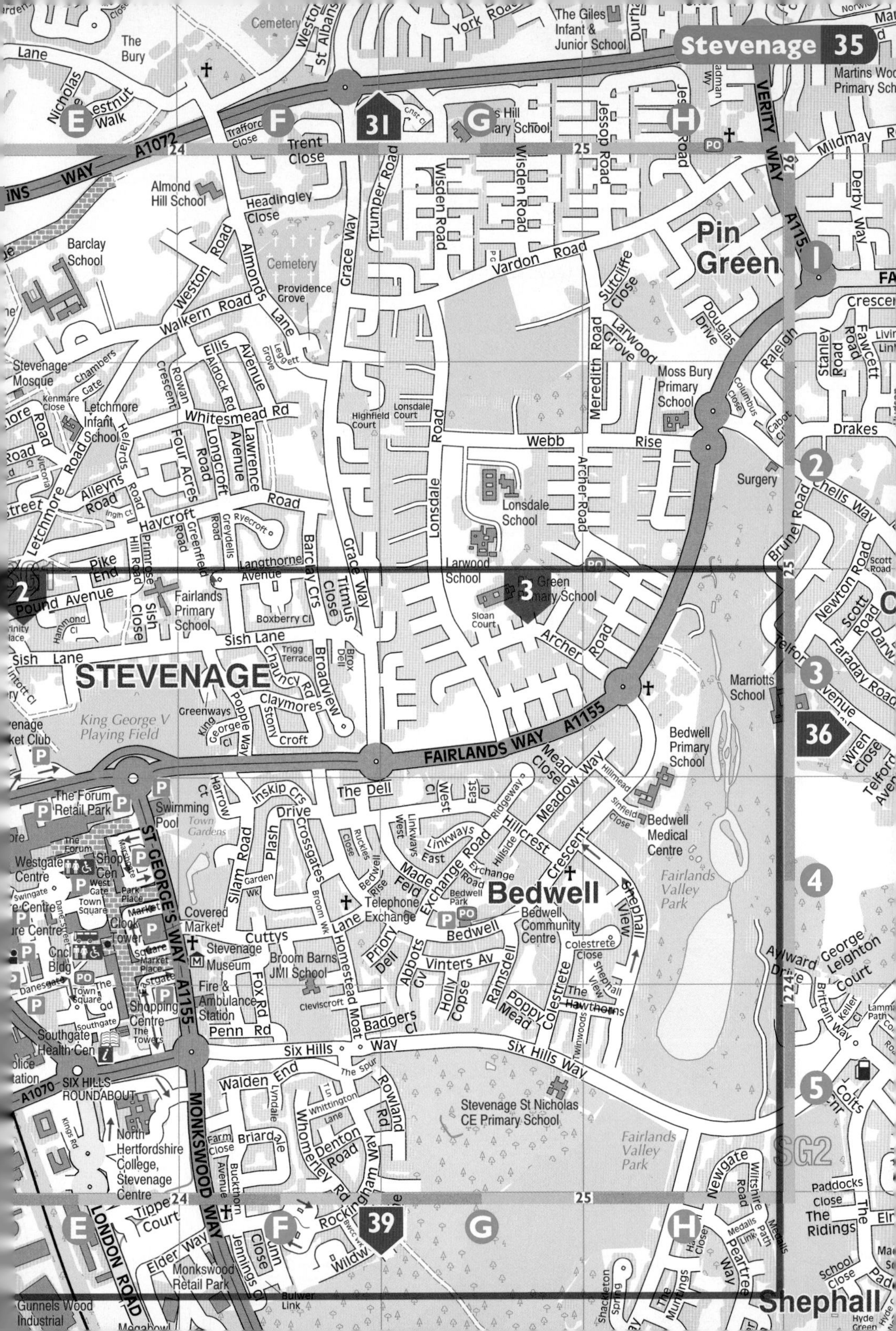

Stevenage 35
31
36
39
2
3
E
F
G
H
I
24
25
26
A1072
A1155
A1070
Pin Green
STEVENAGE
Bedwell
Shephall
SG2
Cemetery
The Bury
The Giles Infant & Junior School
Martins Wood Primary Sch
Almond Hill School
Barclay School
Stevenage Mosque
Letchmore Infant School
Fairlands Primary School
Moss Bury Primary School
Lonsdale School
Larwood School
Pin Green Primary School
Marriotts School
Bedwell Primary School
Bedwell Medical Centre
Surgery
King George V Playing Field
Fairlands Valley Park
Town Gardens
The Forum Retail Park
Swimming Pool
Westgate Centre
Covered Market
Clock Tower
Cncl Bldg
Stevenage Museum
Fire & Ambulance Station
Shopping Centre
Southgate Health Cen
Telephone Exchange
Bedwell Community Centre
Broom Barns JMI School
Stevenage St Nicholas CE Primary School
North Hertfordshire College, Stevenage Centre
Monkswood Retail Park
Gunnels Wood Industrial
SIX HILLS ROUNDABOUT
FAIRLANDS WAY
ST GEORGE'S WAY
MONKSWOOD WAY
LONDON ROAD
VERITY WAY
Six Hills Way
Vardon Road
Walkern Road
Weston Road
Almonds Lane
Grace Way
Trumper Road
Wisden Road
Jessop Road
Lonsdale Road
Webb Rise
Archer Road
Meredith Road
Sutcliffe Close
Larwood Grove
Douglas Drive
Chells Way
Brunel Road
Newton Road
Telford Avenue
Faraday Road
Aylward Drive
George Leighton Court
Whitesmead Rd
Haycroft Road
Sish Lane
Pound Avenue
Letchmore Road
Alleyns Road
Exchange Road
Hillcrest
Meadow Way
Shephall View
Colestrete
Homestead Moat
Badgers Cl
Walden End
Rowland Rd
Whomerley Rd
Denton Road
Rockingham Way
Elder Way
Jennings Cl
Bulwer Link
Newgate
Wiltshire Road
Peartree Way
Mildmay Rd
Derby Way
Drakes
The Ridings

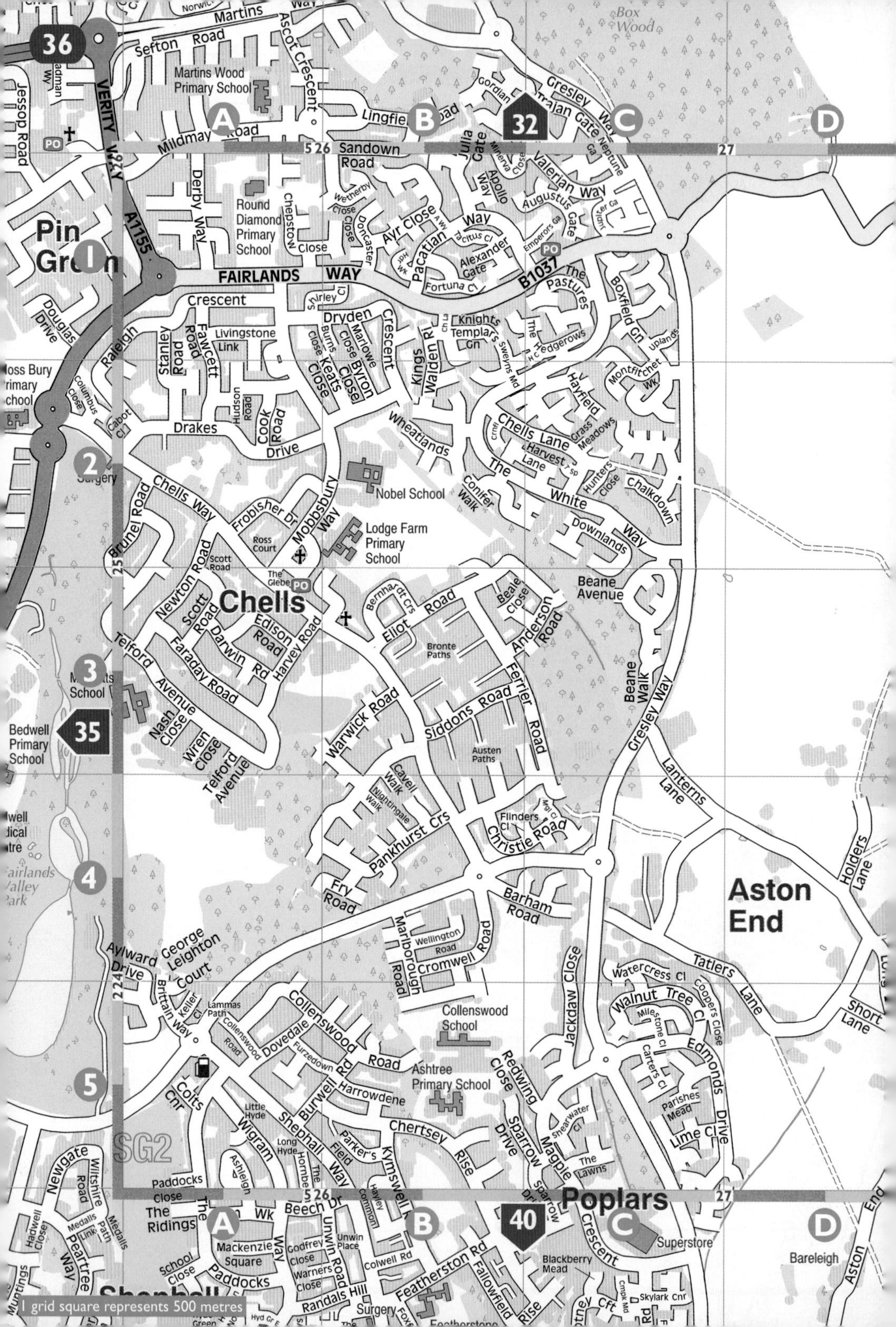
36
32
35
40
A
B
C
D
1
2
3
4
5
526
27
25
224
SG2
Box Wood
Martins
Sefton Road
Ascot Crescent
Jessop Road
VERITY WAY
Martins Wood Primary School
Lingfield Road
Gordian
Gresley Way
Trajan Gate
Neptune Ga
Mildmay Road
Sandown Road
Julia Gate
Minerva Close
Apollo Way
Valerian Way
Augustus Gate
Derby Way
Round Diamond Primary School
Chepstow Close
Wetherby Close
Doncaster Close
Ayr Close
Pacatian Way
Citius Cl
Alexander Gate
Emperors Ga
Fortuna Cl
Pin Green
A1155
FAIRLANDS WAY
B1037
The Pastures
Boxfield Gn
Douglas Drive
Crescent
Shirley Cl
Dryden
Crescent
Knights Templars Gn
The Hedgerows
Uplands
Raleigh
Stanley Road
Fawcett Road
Livingstone Link
Burns Close
Keats Close
Marlowe Close
Byron Close
Kings Walden Ri
Sweyns Md
Montfitchet Wk
Ross Bury Primary School
Columbus Close
Cabot Cl
Hudson Road
Cook Road
Drakes Drive
Wheatlands
Chells Lane
Hayfield
Grass Meadows
Harvest Lane
Surgery
Nobel School
Chells Way
Frobisher Dr
Mobbsbury Way
Conifer Walk
The White Way
Hunters Close
Chalkdown
Downlands
Brunel Road
Ross Court
Lodge Farm Primary School
Newton Road
Scott Road
The Glebe
PO
Chells
Beale Close
Anderson Road
Beane Avenue
Bernhardt Crs
Eliot Road
Edison Road
Harvey Road
Darwin Rd
Faraday Road
Telford Avenue
Bronte Paths
Ferrier Road
Siddons Road
Beane Walk
Gresley Way
Nash Close
Wren Close
Warwick Road
Austen Paths
Bedwell Primary School
Cavell Walk
Nightingale Walk
Lanterns Lane
Flinders Cl
Christie Road
Pankhurst Crs
Fairlands Valley Park
Holders Lane
Fry Road
Barham Road
Aston End
Marlborough Road
Wellington Road
Cromwell Road
Jackdaw Close
Watercress Cl
Tatlers Lane
George Leighton Court
Aylward Drive
Brittain Way
Keller Cl
Lammas Path
Collenswood Road
Collenswood Road
Dovedale
Furzedown
Collenswood School
Walnut Tree Cl
Milestone Cl
Coopers Close
Short Lane
Ashtree Primary School
Redwing Close
Carters Cl
Edmonds Drive
Burwell Rd
Harrowdene
Colts Cnr
Little Hyde
Wigram
Shephall Way
Parishes Mead
Shearwater Cl
Chertsey Rise
Sparrow Drive
Magpie
Lime Cl
Long Hyde
Field
Parker's
Kymswell
The Lawns
Newgate
Wiltshire Road
Ashleigh
Paddocks Close
The Ridings
Beech Dr
Hayley Common
Poplars
Crescent
Medalls Link
Medalls Path
Hadwell Close
Peartree Way
Mackenzie Square
Godfrey Close
Unwin Road
Unwin Place
Colwell Rd
Featherston Rd
Fallowfield
Superstore
Bareleigh
Aston End
School Close
Paddocks
Warners Close
Blackberry Mead
Randals Hill
Surgery
Skylark Cnr
Rise
1 grid square represents 500 metres

Walkern
Froghall Lane
Brockwell Shott
HIGH ST
Totts Lane
Lane
PO
33
Moors Ley
Aubries
Rise
E
F
G
H
I
28
29
26
25
224
STEVENAGE ROAD B1037
Finches End
The Maltings
Street
Wrights Meadow
Greenway
High
River Beane
Benington Road
Walkern Road
2
3
SG2
4
Box Hall
Lordship Farm
Lordship
5
Lordship Gardens
High Wood
Brookfield Lane
Town Lane
41

Dyes Lane
A
B
34
C
D
Stevenage Leisure Park
Caxton Way
Potters Lane
Chadwell Road
SIX H
522
23
Six Hills Way
Norton
GUNNELS
Dyes Lane
Norton Green
Factory
1
Dyes Farm
A1(M)
23
2
gleyhill
Village St
Homefield Lane
3
Langley
Newton Wood
22
4
Burleigh Farm
B656
Graffridge Wood
5
221
522
23
A
B
42
C
D
Old Knebworth
Knebworth House, Gardens & Country Park
1 grid square represents 500 metres

Broadwater 39
Stevenage St Nicholas CE Primary School
Fairlands Valley Park
North Hertfordshire College, Stevenage Centre
SIX HILLS ROUNDABOUT
MONKSWOOD WAY
LONDON ROAD
Monkswood Retail Park
Gunnels Wood Industrial Estate
Megabowl
Roaring Meg Retail Park
BROADHALL WAY
A602
Junction 7
Stevenage Borough FC
St Margaret Clitherow RC Primary School
Roebuck JMI School
Roebuck Retail Park
Monks View
Heathcote School
Shephall Green Infant School
Greenside Special School
Shephall
Broadwater
Burydale Junior School
Marymead Industrial Estate
Hotel
Golf Course
Knebworth Golf Club
STEVENAGE ROAD
B197
A1(M)
Badger Close
Oakfields Avenue
Deard's End Lane
Kimbolton Crescent
Broadwater Crescent
Hertford Road
Tintern Close
Braemar Close
35
3
40
43

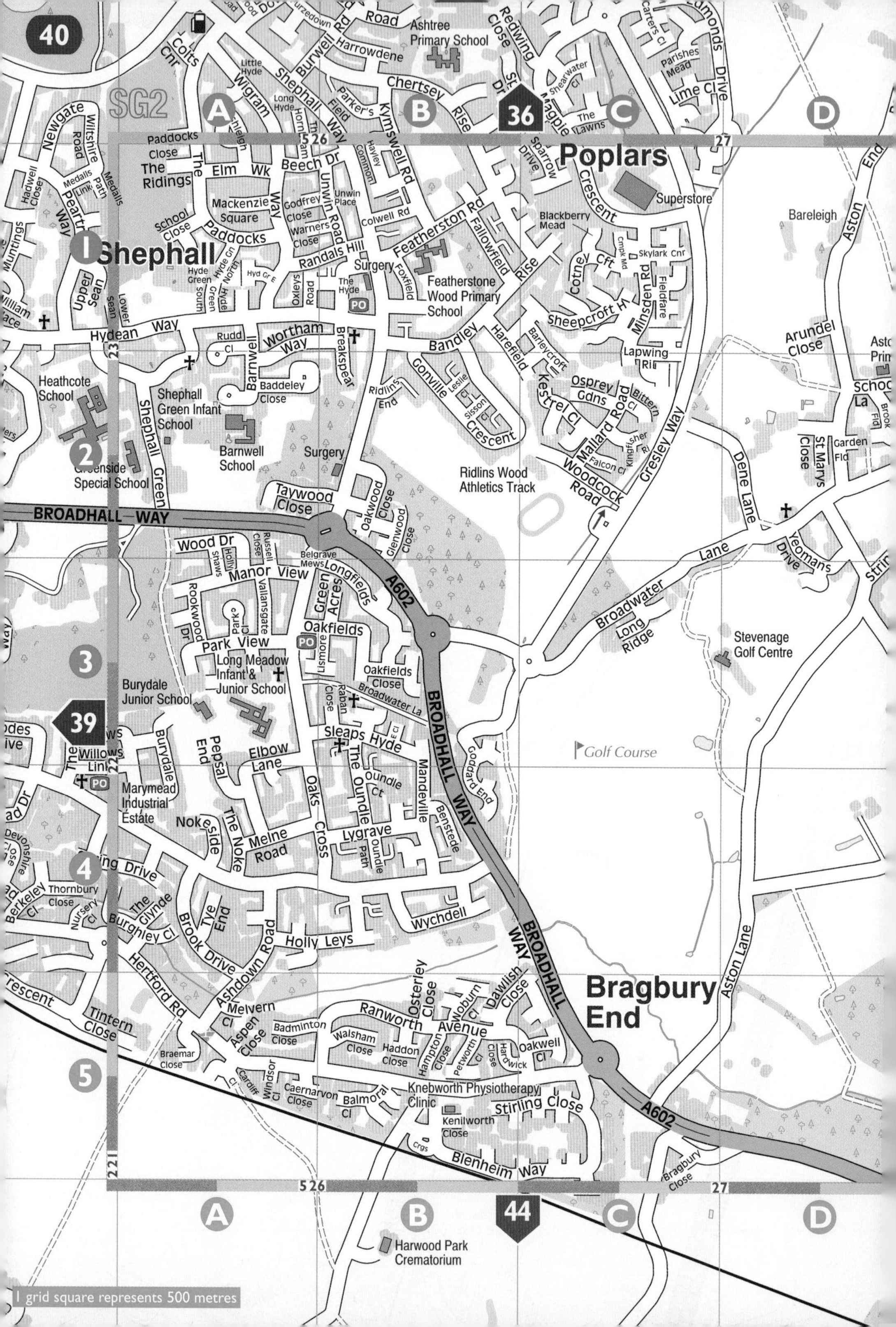

40
SG2
Road
Ashtree Primary School
Harrowdene
Burwell Rd
Shephall Way
Colts Cnr
Little Hyde
Wigram
Long Hyde
Chertsey Rise
Parker's Field
Kymswell Rd
Redwing Close
St Dr
Magpie
Shearwater Cl
Carters Cl
Parishes Mead
Lime Cl
Edmonds Drive
The Lawns
36
A
B
C
D
Newgate
Wiltshire Road
Paddocks Close
526
27
The Ridings
Elm Wk
Beech Dr
Unwin Road
Hayley Common
Sparrow Drive
Poplars
Superstore
Crescent
Medalls Link
Medalls Path
Medalls
Hadwell Close
Peartree Way
Mackenzie Square
Godfrey Close
Unwin Place
Colwell Rd
Featherston Rd
Fallowfield
Blackberry Mead
Bareleigh
Aston End
Muntings
School Close
Paddocks
Warners Close
Randals Hill
Cotney Cft
Skylark Cnr
1
Shephall
Hyde Green South
Hyde Green
Hyde Green North
Hyd Gr E
Oxleys Road
Surgery
The Hyde
PO
Foxfield
Featherstone Wood Primary School
Rise
Minsden Rd
Fieldfare
Sheepcroft H
Upper Sean
Lower Sean
William
Hydean Way
Rudd Cl
Wortham Way
Barnwell
Breakspear
Bandley
Harefield
Barleycroft
Lapwing Ri
Arundel Close
23
Heathcote School
Shephall Green Infant School
Baddeley Close
Ridlins End
Gonville Crescent
Leslie Cl
Sisson Cl
Osprey Gdns
Kestrel Cl
Bittern Cl
Mallard Road
Gresley Way
School La
Brook Fld
Garden Fld
St Marys Close
2
Greenside Special School
Shephall Green
Barnwell School
Surgery
Falcon Cl
Kingfisher Ri
Woodcock Road
Ridlins Wood Athletics Track
Dene Lane
Taywood Close
Oakwood Close
Glenwood Close
BROADHALL WAY
Wood Dr
Holly Shaws
Russell Close
Belgrave Mews
Longfields
A602
Yeomans Drive
Lane
Broadwater
Long Ridge
Manor View
Rookwood Dr
Vallansgate
Park Cl
Green Acres
Oakfields
Stevenage Golf Centre
3
Park View
Long Meadow Infant & Junior School
Lismore
Oakfields Close
Burydale Junior School
Raban Close
Broadwater La
BROADHALL WAY
39
The Willows
Willows Link
Burydale
Pepsal End
Elbow Lane
Sleaps Hyde
The Oundle
Oundle Ct
Mandeville
Goddard End
Golf Course
Marymead Industrial Estate
Nokeside
The Noke
Oaks Cross
Melne Road
Lygrave
Oundle Path
Benstede
Devonshire Close
4
Thornbury Close
Berkeley Cl
Nursery Cl
The Glynde
Tye End
Brook Drive
Ashdown Road
Burghley Cl
Holly Leys
Wychdell
Hertford Rd
Crescent
Tintern Close
Melvern Cl
Aspen Close
Badminton Close
Ranworth Avenue
Osterley Close
Woburn Cl
Dawlish Close
BROADHALL WAY
Bragbury End
Aston Lane
Walsham Close
Haddon Close
Hampton Close
Petworth Cl
Hardwick Close
Oakwell Cl
5
Braemar Close
Cardiff Cl
Windsor Cl
Caernarvon Close
Balmoral Cl
Knebworth Physiotherapy Clinic
Kenilworth Close
Stirling Close
Crgs
Blenheim Way
Bragbury Close
A602
221
44
Harwood Park Crematorium
1 grid square represents 500 metres

Brookfield
E
F
37
High Wood
G
H
28
29
Town Lane
1
23
Aston
ington Road
2
Holbrook Farm
3
River Beane
22
White Hall
4
5
Astonbury Wood
Leatherfield Common
221
28
29
E
F
45
G
H
Frogmore
Walkern Road
Hook's Cross
Frogmore Hall

42
38
A
B
C
D
522
23
21
20
219
1
2
3
4
5
Old Knebworth
Knebworth House, Gardens & Country Park
Manor Way
The Green
PH
Park Lane
Slip Lane
The Node
Driver's End Lane
Driver's End
Nup End
Nup End Industrial Est
Business Centre
Sally
Dearids Lane
Plummer's Farm
Mansells Farm
B656
Mansells La
Bury Lane
Rabley Heath Road
Ra
Tower Road
St Giles Road
The Elms
Bentick Way
Gomer Close
The Chestnuts
School Close
Old
Hillside
Grange Rise
Valley Road
The Ridge
The Close
Codico
Potte
New
Road
PO
1 grid square represents 500 metres

Golf Course
KNEBWORTH
Knebworth Golf Club
Lodge Farm
ebworth
Park Lane
Deard's End Lane
Stobarts Close
Deards Wood
Keiths Wood
Dancote
Station Ap
Peters Way
Kerr Close
New Close
Westland Road
Knebworth Station
Station Rd
Badger Close
Oakfields Avenue
Oakfields Road
Bell Close
Watton Road
Old Lane
LONDON ROAD
St Martin's Road
Swangley's Lane
Swangley's
Milestone Road
Pondcroft Road
Gun Lane
Gipsy Lane
Orchard Way
Bellamy Close
Lytton Fields
Deanscroft
Broom Grove
Stonecroft
Gibbons Wy
Stockens Dell
Hornbeam Spring
Sayer Way
Stockens Gn
Stockens Green
Haygarth
Gun Rd
Gn M Av
Cherry Close
Wadnall Way
Meadway
Gun Road Gardens
Crab Tree Road
Woodstock
Cemetery
New Wood
A1(M)
B197
Wych Elm Lane
Works
Spinney Lane
Darby Drive
Normans Lane
Ninning's Lane
eath
Wickfield Close
Longmead
Garden Road
Bridge Road
Hall Lane
Evergreen Cl
Wolves Mere
Mayshades Close
Carvers Croft
Win Foxes
Mardlebury Road
Holly Road
Birchbury Road
Oak Road
Broadfield Road
Wo Gre
Mardley Heath
Heath Road
The Drive
Pottersheath Road
Fallow End
th
E
F
G
H
I
2
3
4
5
24
25
19
20
21
39
44

KNEBWORTH
Woolmer Green
Mardlebury
Painter's Green
Datch
Datchworth Green
Harwood Park Crematorium
Knebworth Physiotherapy Clinic
Swangley's Farm
Bury Farm
Datchworth School
Works
SG3
A602
Blenheim Way
Stirling Close
Kenilworth Close
Balmoral Cl
Caernarvon Close
Windsor Cl
Cardiff Cl
Braemar Close
Haddon Close
Petworth Cl
Hardwick Close
Oakwell Cl
Bragbury Close
Bragbury Lane
Watton Road
Bell Close
Old Lane
St Martin's Road
Swangley's Lane
Haygarth
Baines Lane
Bury Lane
Hollybush Lane
New Road
Rectory Lane
Garden Road
London Road
Longmead
Hall Lane
Evergreen Cl
Mayshades Close
Carvers Croft
Wolves Mere
Twin Foxes
Mardlebury Road
Holly Road
Birch Road
Oak Road
Broadfield Road
Wheatcotes
Foldingshott
Raffin Close
Raffin Park
Raffin Green
Brookbridge Lane
Nutcroft
Great Lawne
Meadow Close
Pn Cl
Hawkins Hall Lane
Abbots Close
Haw Farm
40
43
1 grid square represents 500 metres

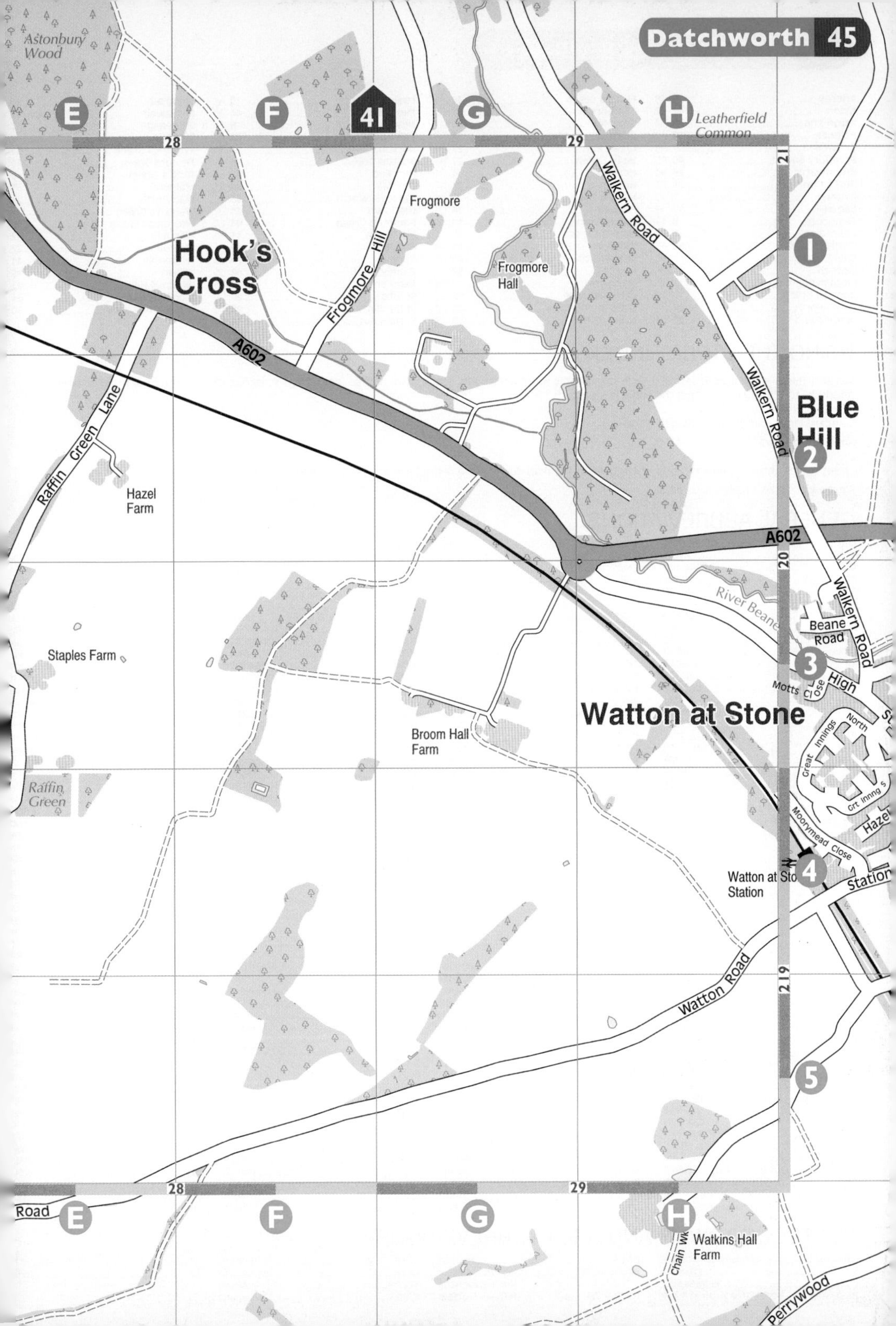
Astonbury Wood
E
F
41
G
H
Leatherfield Common
28
29
21
Frogmore
Walkern Road
Hook's Cross
Frogmore Hill
Frogmore Hall
I
A602
Raffin Green Lane
Walkern Road
Blue Hill
2
Hazel Farm
A602
20
River Beane
Walkern Road
Beane Road
Staples Farm
3
Motts Close
High
Watton at Stone
Broom Hall Farm
Great Innings North
Grt Innng S
Hazel
Raffin Green
Moorymead Close
4
Watton at Sto
Station
Station
Watton Road
219
5
28
29
Road
E
F
G
H
Chain Wk
Watkins Hall Farm
Perrywood

USING THE STREET INDEX

Street names are listed alphabetically. Each street name is followed by its postal town or area locality, the Postcode District, the page number, and the reference to the square in which the name is found.

Standard index entries are shown as follows:

Abbis Orch *HTCH/STOT* SG5 ....**17** F3

Street names and selected addresses not shown on the map due to scale restrictions are shown in the index with an asterisk:

Alexander Ct *BLDK* * SG7..................**14** B5

GENERAL ABBREVIATIONS

ACC	ACCESS
ALY	ALLEY
AP	APPROACH
AR	ARCADE
ASS	ASSOCIATION
AV	AVENUE
BCH	BEACH
BLDS	BUILDINGS
BND	BEND
BNK	BANK
BR	BRIDGE
BRK	BROOK
BTM	BOTTOM
BUS	BUSINESS
BVD	BOULEVARD
BY	BYPASS
CATH	CATHEDRAL
CEM	CEMETERY
CEN	CENTRE
CFT	CROFT
CH	CHURCH
CHA	CHASE
CHYD	CHURCHYARD
CIR	CIRCLE
CIRC	CIRCUS
CL	CLOSE
CLFS	CLIFFS
CMP	CAMP
CNR	CORNER
CO	COUNTY
COLL	COLLEGE
COM	COMMON
COMM	COMMISSION
CON	CONVENT
COT	COTTAGE
COTS	COTTAGES
CP	CAPE
CPS	COPSE
CR	CREEK
CREM	CREMATORIUM
CRS	CRESCENT
CSWY	CAUSEWAY
CT	COURT
CTRL	CENTRAL
CTS	COURTS
CTYD	COURTYARD
CUTT	CUTTINGS
CV	COVE
CYN	CANYON
DEPT	DEPARTMENT
DL	DALE
DM	DAM
DR	DRIVE
DRO	DROVE
DRY	DRIVEWAY
DWGS	DWELLINGS
E	EAST
EMB	EMBANKMENT
EMBY	EMBASSY
ESP	ESPLANADE
EST	ESTATE
EX	EXCHANGE
EXPY	EXPRESSWAY
EXT	EXTENSION
F/O	FLYOVER
FC	FOOTBALL CLUB
FK	FORK
FLD	FIELD
FLDS	FIELDS
FLS	FALLS
FLS	FLATS
FM	FARM
FT	FORT
FWY	FREEWAY
FY	FERRY
GA	GATE
GAL	GALLERY
GDN	GARDEN
GDNS	GARDENS
GLD	GLADE
GLN	GLEN
GN	GREEN
GND	GROUND
GRA	GRANGE
GRG	GARAGE
GT	GREAT
GTWY	GATEWAY
GV	GROVE
HGR	HIGHER
HL	HILL
HLS	HILLS
HO	HOUSE
HOL	HOLLOW
HOSP	HOSPITAL
HRB	HARBOUR
HTH	HEATH
HTS	HEIGHTS
HVN	HAVEN
HWY	HIGHWAY
IMP	IMPERIAL
IN	INLET
IND EST	INDUSTRIAL ESTATE
INF	INFIRMARY
INFO	INFORMATION
INT	INTERCHANGE
IS	ISLAND
JCT	JUNCTION
JTY	JETTY
KG	KING
KNL	KNOLL
L	LAKE
LA	LANE
LDG	LODGE
LGT	LIGHT
LK	LOCK
LKS	LAKES
LNDG	LANDING
LTL	LITTLE
LWR	LOWER
MAG	MAGISTRATE
MAN	MANSIONS
MD	MEAD
MDW	MEADOWS
MEM	MEMORIAL
MKT	MARKET
MKTS	MARKETS
ML	MALL
ML	MILL
MNR	MANOR
MS	MEWS
MSN	MISSION
MT	MOUNT
MTN	MOUNTAIN
MTS	MOUNTAINS
MUS	MUSEUM
MWY	MOTORWAY
N	NORTH
NE	NORTH EAST
NW	NORTH WEST
O/P	OVERPASS
OFF	OFFICE
ORCH	ORCHARD
OV	OVAL
PAL	PALACE
PAS	PASSAGE
PAV	PAVILION
PDE	PARADE
PH	PUBLIC HOUSE
PK	PARK
PKWY	PARKWAY
PL	PLACE
PLN	PLAIN
PLNS	PLAINS
PLZ	PLAZA
POL	POLICE STATION
PR	PRINCE
PREC	PRECINCT
PREP	PREPARATORY
PRIM	PRIMARY
PROM	PROMENADE
PRS	PRINCESS
PRT	PORT
PT	POINT
PTH	PATH
PZ	PIAZZA
QD	QUADRANT
QU	QUEEN
QY	QUAY
R	RIVE
RBT	ROUNDABOU
RD	ROA
RDG	RIDG
REP	REPUBLI
RES	RESERVO
RFC	RUGBY FOOTBALL CLU
RI	RIS
RP	RAM
RW	ROW
S	SOUT
SCH	SCHOO
SE	SOUTH EAS
SER	SERVICE ARE
SH	SHOR
SHOP	SHOPPIN
SKWY	SKYWA
SMT	SUMM
SOC	SOCIET
SP	SPU
SPR	SPRIN
SQ	SQUAR
ST	STREE
STN	STATIO
STR	STREA
STRD	STRAN
SW	SOUTH WES
TDG	TRADIN
TER	TERRAC
THWY	THROUGHWA
TNL	TUNNE
TOLL	TOLLWA
TPK	TURNPIK
TR	TRAC
TRL	TRA
TWR	TOWE
U/P	UNDERPAS
UNI	UNIVERSIT
UPR	UPPE
V	VA
VA	VALL
VIAD	VIADU
VIL	VIL
VIS	VIST
VLG	VILLAG
VLS	VILL
VW	VIE
W	WE
WD	WOO
WHF	WHA
WK	WA
WKS	WAL
WLS	WEL
WY	WA
YD	YAR
YHA	YOUTH HOST

POSTCODE TOWNS AND AREA ABBREVIATIONS

ARL/CHE	Arlesey/Church End
BLDK	Baldock
BGSW	Biggleswade
HERT/WAS	Hertford/Watton at Stone
HNLW	Henlow
HTCHE/RSTV	Hitchin East/ Rural Stevenage
HTCH/STOT	Hitchin/Stotfold
KNEB	Knebworth
LWTH	Letchworth
SHFD	Shefford
STVG	Stevenage
STVGE	Stevenage e
WLYN	Welv

A

s Orch HTCH/STOT SG5 17 F3
ots Gv STVG SG1 3 G4
otts Rd LWTH SG6 18 C2
Piece HTCHE/RSTV SG4 23 H5
ngton Cl HNLW SG16 5 E1
ger Cl STVG SG1 3 F7
ree Wy STVGE SG2 36 B1
n Rd LWTH SG6 19 H5
rt Rd ARL/CHE SG15 11 H1
rt St STVG SG1 34 D2
burgh Cl STVG SG1 30 B5
r Cl BLDK SG7 20 B1
ck Rd STVG SG1 35 F1
idge Ct BLDK SG7 14 B4
ander Ct BLDK * SG7 14 B5
ander Ga STVGE SG2 36 B1
ander Rd HTCH/STOT SG5 7 E4
andra Rd HTCH/STOT SG5 23 G2
n Wy BLDK SG7 15 E4
gton La LWTH SG6 19 E5
yns Rd STVG SG1 35 E2
on Rd HNLW SG16 10 B1
onds La STVG SG1 35 F1
ne Cl HTCHE/RSTV SG4 28 D1
or Wy LWTH SG6 19 G2
hor Rd BLDK SG7 20 C1
erson Rd STVGE SG2 36 B3
le Ways STVGE SG2 39 G2
otts Md STVG SG1 34 C3
llo Wy STVG SG1 36 B1
lecroft HNLW SG16 10 B2
letrees HTCH/STOT * SG5 23 E5
ner Rd STVG SG1 3 H1
ners Wy LWTH SG6 18 C2
Arches LWTH SG6 19 F1
n Rd HTCHE/RSTV SG4 29 G2
en Press Wy LWTH SG6 19 G2
yle Wy STVG SG1 2 A3
sey New Rd LWTH SG6 18 B1
sey Rd HNLW SG16 5 E2
TCH/STOT SG5 6 C4
TCH/STOT SG5 17 F4
our Ri HTCHE/RSTV SG4 24 A1
old Cl HTCHE/RSTV SG4 24 A3
VG SG1 31 E5
hur Gibbons Ct STVG * SG1 31 H5
ndel Cl STVGE SG2 40 D1
ot Crs STVG SG1 32 A5
anger La BLDK SG7 21 G4
bourne Cl LWTH SG6 19 G4
brook La HTCHE/RSTV SG4 29 F2
burnam Wk STVGE SG2 39 G3
down LWTH SG6 12 D4
down Rd STVGE SG2 40 A5
Dr HTCHE/RSTV SG4 28 D2
leigh STVGE SG2 36 A5
ton's La BLDK SG7 20 B2
ville Wy BLDK SG7 14 D4
well Cl HTCHE/RSTV SG4 30 C2
well Common
TCHE/RSTV SG4 30 C2
well Rd BLDK SG7 8 C2
LDK SG7 15 E3
en Cl STVGE SG2 40 A5
Aspens HTCHE/RSTV SG4 23 H5
on End Rd STVGE SG2 40 D1
on La STVGE SG2 40 D5
on Ri HTCHE/RSTV SG4 24 A5
al Cl HNLW SG16 10 C1
wick Rd HTCH/STOT SG5 6 D1
reys LWTH SG6 25 E1
ries STVGE SG2 37 G1
ustus Ga STVGE SG2 36 B1
ten Paths STVGE SG2 36 B3
nue One LWTH SG6 19 H2
Avenue HTCH/STOT SG5 7 E4
TCHE/RSTV SG4 23 H4
VG SG1 34 D1
cet LWTH SG6 12 D4
n Rd HNLW SG16 10 C1
Cl STVGE SG2 36 B1

B

bage Rd STVG SG1 34 C4
deley Cl STVGE SG2 40 A2
er Cl STVG SG1 31 F5
ger Cl KNEB SG3 43 G1
gers Cl STVG SG1 3 F5
minton Cl STVGE SG2 40 A5
nes La KNEB SG3 44 B4
er St STVG SG1 34 D2
Baldock La LWTH SG6 25 G1
Baldock Rd HTCH/STOT SG5 7 F5
LWTH SG6 19 G3
Baliol Rd HTCH/STOT SG5 23 G3
Balmoral Cl STVGE SG2 40 B5
Balmoral Rd HTCH/STOT SG5 23 F2
Bancroft HTCH/STOT SG5 23 G4
Bandley Ri STVGE SG2 40 B1
Barclay Crs STVG SG1 35 F2
Barham Rd STVGE SG2 36 B4
Barley Cft KNEB * SG3 43 H5
Barleycroft STVGE SG2 40 C1
Barley Ri BLDK SG7 15 E5
Barndell Cl HTCH/STOT SG5 7 E4
Barnwell STVGE SG2 40 A2
Baron Ct STVG SG1 30 C5
Barrington Rd LWTH SG6 19 E4
Basils Rd STVG SG1 34 D2
Bawdsey Cl STVG SG1 34 C1
Bayworth LWTH SG6 19 G3
Beale Cl STVGE SG2 36 B3
Beane Av STVGE SG2 36 C3
Beane Wk STVGE SG2 36 C3
Bearton Av HTCH/STOT SG5 23 F3
Bearton Gn HTCH/STOT SG5 23 E2
Bearton Rd HTCH/STOT SG5 23 F2
Bedford Rd HTCH/STOT SG5 16 D1
HTCH/STOT SG5 17 E5
HTCH/STOT SG5 23 E2
LWTH SG6 18 C1
Bedwell Crs STVG SG1 3 F3
Bedwell Pk STVG SG1 3 G4
Bedwell Ri STVG SG1 3 F4
Beech Dr STVGE SG2 40 A1
The Beeches HTCHE/RSTV SG4 23 H5
Beech Hl LWTH SG6 18 C1
Beechwood Cl BLDK SG7 20 C3
HTCH/STOT SG5 23 E1
Beecroft La STVGE SG2 33 G4
Belgrave Ms STVGE SG2 40 A2
Bell Acre LWTH SG6 19 G4
Bell Acre Gdns LWTH SG6 19 G4
Bellamy Cl KNEB SG3 43 G2
Bell Cl HTCHE/RSTV SG4 24 A5
KNEB SG3 43 H2
Bell La STVG SG1 34 D2
Bell Rw BLDK SG7 14 B5
Benchley Hl HTCHE/RSTV SG4 24 B3
Benington Rd STVGE SG2 37 F3
STVGE SG2 41 E2
Bennett Ct LWTH SG6 19 F3
Benslow La HTCHE/RSTV SG4 23 H4
Benslow Ri HTCHE/RSTV SG4 23 H4
Benstede STVGE SG2 40 B4
Bentick Wy HTCHE/RSTV SG4 42 A5
Berkeley LWTH SG6 19 F4
Berkeley Cl STVGE SG2 39 H4
Bernhardt Crs STVGE SG2 36 B3
Berwick Cl STVG SG1 34 B1
Bessemer Cl HTCH/STOT SG5 23 F1
Bessemer Dr STVG SG1 34 C5
Beverley Rd STVG SG1 32 A4
Bidwell Cl LWTH SG6 19 G3
Biggin La HTCH/STOT SG5 23 F4
Bilton Rd HTCHE/RSTV SG4 23 G1
Bingen Rd HTCH/STOT SG5 22 D2
The Birches LWTH SG6 12 D5
Birds Hl LWTH SG6 19 F2
Bittern Cl STVGE SG2 40 C2
Bittern Wy LWTH SG6 12 D4
Blackberry Md STVGE SG2 40 C1
Blackdown Cl STVG SG1 32 A3
Blackhorse Cl HTCHE/RSTV SG4 28 D1
Blackhorse La HTCHE/RSTV SG4 28 D2
Blackhorse Rd LWTH SG6 13 H5
Blackmore LWTH SG6 19 G5
Bladon Cl HTCHE/RSTV SG4 30 A3
Blair Cl STVGE SG2 39 G3
Blakemore End Rd
HTCHE/RSTV SG4 29 G3
Blakeney Rd STVG SG1 34 B2
Blenheim Wy KNEB SG3 40 B5
Blyth Cl STVG SG1 34 B2
Bockings STVGE SG2 33 H5
Borton Av HNLW SG16 10 C1
Boscombe Ct LWTH * SG6 19 G3
Boswell Dr HTCH/STOT SG5 17 F4
Boswell Gdns STVG SG1 31 E5
Boulton Rd STVG SG1 32 B4
Bournemouth Rd STVG SG1 34 C1
Bowcock Wk STVG SG1 3 F7
Bowershott LWTH SG6 19 F4
Bowling Gn STVG SG1 34 D2
Bowmans Av HTCHE/RSTV SG4 24 A4
Bowyer's Cl HTCH/STOT SG5 23 E2
Boxberry Cl STVG SG1 2 E1
Boxfield Gn STVGE SG2 36 C1
Bradford St HTCH/STOT SG5 23 E4
Bradleys Cnr HTCHE/RSTV SG4 24 B3
Bradman Wy STVG SG1 31 H5
Bradshaw Ct STVGE * SG2 40 A1
Braemar Cl KNEB SG3 40 A5
Bragbury Cl STVGE SG2 40 C5
Bragbury La KNEB SG3 44 B3
The Brambles STVG SG1 31 E4
Bramfield HTCHE/RSTV SG4 24 A5
Bramley Cl BLDK SG7 14 C4
Brampton Park Rd
HTCH/STOT SG5 23 F2
Bramshott Cl HTCHE/RSTV SG4 28 C2
Brandles Rd LWTH SG6 19 F5
Brand St HTCH/STOT SG5 23 F4
Brayes Mnr HTCH/STOT SG5 7 E4
Breakspear STVGE SG2 40 B1
Brewery La BLDK SG7 14 B4
Briardale STVG SG1 2 E6
Briar Patch La LWTH SG6 18 C5
Brick Kiln La HTCH/STOT SG5 28 B1
Brickkiln Rd STVG SG1 2 A2
Bridge Rd KNEB SG3 43 H5
LWTH SG6 19 E2
Bridge Rd West STVG SG1 34 C3
Bridge St HTCH/STOT SG5 23 F5
Brighton Wy STVG SG1 34 B1
Brittain Wy STVGE SG2 36 A4
Brixham Cl STVG SG1 34 C2
Broadcroft LWTH SG6 25 E1
Broadhall Wy STVGE SG2 39 H2
Broadmead HTCHE/RSTV SG4 28 D1
Broadmeadow Ride
HTCHE/RSTV SG4 28 D2
Broad Oak Wy STVGE SG2 39 G3
Broadview STVG SG1 3 F2
Broadwater Av LWTH SG6 18 D3
Broadwater Crs STVGE SG2 39 G3
Broadwater Dl LWTH SG6 18 D3
Broadwater La STVGE SG2 40 B3
Broadway LWTH SG6 18 D5
Brockwell Shott STVGE SG2 33 G5
Bronte Paths STVGE SG2 36 B3
Brookbridge La KNEB SG3 44 C5
Brook Cl HNLW SG16 5 E1
Brook Dr STVGE SG2 40 A4
Brook Fld STVGE SG2 40 D2
Brookfield La STVGE SG2 37 E5
Brookhill STVGE SG2 39 G4
Brookside LWTH * SG6 19 E3
Brook St HTCH/STOT SG5 6 D4
Brook Vw HTCHE/RSTV SG4 24 B5
Broom Gv KNEB SG3 43 G2
Broom Wk STVG SG1 3 F4
Broughton Hl LWTH SG6 19 F2
Browning Dr HTCHE/RSTV SG4 24 A3
Brox Dell STVG SG1 3 F1
Brunel Rd STVGE SG2 35 H2
Bucklersbury HTCH/STOT SG5 23 F5
Buckthorn Av STVG SG1 2 E6
Bude Crs STVG SG1 34 B3
Bulwer Link STVG SG1 2 E7
Bunyan Rd HTCH/STOT SG5 23 F3
Burford Wy HTCH/STOT SG5 22 D1
Burghley Cl STVGE SG2 39 H4
Burley LWTH SG6 13 E4
Burnell Ri LWTH SG6 18 C3
Burnell Wk LWTH SG6 18 D3
Burnett Av HNLW SG16 10 C1
Burns Cl HTCHE/RSTV SG4 24 A3
STVGE SG2 36 A1
Bursland LWTH SG6 18 C2
Burwell Rd STVGE SG2 36 A5
Burydale STVGE SG2 40 A3
Bury La KNEB SG3 44 C4
Bury Md ARL/CHE SG15 5 H3
Burymead STVG SG1 30 D5
Bury Mead Rd HTCH/STOT SG5 23 G1
Bush Spring BLDK SG7 14 D4
Butlers Yd BLDK * SG7 14 C4
Butts Gn HTCHE/RSTV * SG4 27 F2
Bygrave Rd BLDK SG7 14 C4
Byrd Wk BLDK SG7 20 C2
Byron Cl HTCHE/RSTV SG4 24 A3
STVGE SG2 36 B2

C

Cabot Cl STVGE SG2 35 H2
Cade Cl LWTH SG6 13 H4
Cadwell La HTCH/STOT SG5 23 G1
Caernarvon Cl STVGE SG2 40 A5
Caister Cl STVG SG1 30 B5
Caldecote Rd BLDK SG7 8 A1
California BLDK SG7 14 C4
Cambridge Rd HTCHE/RSTV SG4 24 A2
Cam Centre HTCHE/RSTV * SG4 17 H5
Campbell Cl HTCHE/RSTV SG4 24 A3
Campers Av LWTH SG6 18 D3
Campers Rd LWTH SG6 18 C3
Campers Wk LWTH SG6 18 D3
Campfield Wy LWTH SG6 18 B3
Campkin Md STVGE SG2 40 C1
Campus Five LWTH SG6 19 H1
Cam Sq HTCHE/RSTV * SG4 17 H5
Cannix Cl STVGE SG2 39 H2
Canterbury Wy STVG SG1 31 G4
Cardiff Cl STVGE SG2 40 A5
Carters Cl ARL/CHE SG15 5 H3
STVGE SG2 36 C5
Carters La (Wibbly Wobbley La)
HTCH/STOT SG5 22 B4
Carters Wy ARL/CHE SG15 5 H3
Cartwright Rd STVG SG1 32 B4
Cashio La LWTH SG6 13 F4
Caslon Wy LWTH SG6 13 E4
Castle Ct HTCH/STOT SG5 23 E2
Castles Cl HTCH/STOT SG5 7 E3
Cavell Wk STVGE SG2 36 B3
Cavendish Rd STVG SG1 34 B3
Caxton Ga STVG * SG1 34 C5
Caxton Pl STVG * SG1 34 C5
Caxton Wy STVG SG1 34 C5
Cedar Av HTCH/STOT SG5 17 F4
Central Av HNLW SG16 10 C2
The Chace STVGE SG2 39 G3
Chadwell Rd STVG SG1 34 C5
Chagny Cl LWTH SG6 18 D2
Chalkdown STVGE SG2 36 C2
Chalk Fld LWTH SG6 19 H5
Chalk Hills BLDK SG7 20 C3
Chambers Ga STVG SG1 35 E2
Chambers La HTCH/STOT SG5 17 F4
Chancellors Rd STVG SG1 30 D5
Chantry La HTCHE/RSTV SG4 30 A4
Chaomans LWTH SG6 19 E5
Chapel Pl HTCH/STOT SG5 7 E5
Chapel Rw HTCH/STOT * SG5 23 G3
Chapman Rd STVG SG1 30 C5
The Chapmans
HTCH/STOT * SG5 23 F5
Charlton Rd HTCH/STOT SG5 28 A1
Chase Cl ARL/CHE SG15 5 H2
Chase Hill Rd ARL/CHE SG15 5 H3
Chasten Hl LWTH SG6 18 C1
Chatsworth Ct STVGE SG2 39 G3
Chatterton LWTH SG6 19 G3
Chaucer Wy HTCHE/RSTV SG4 24 B4
Chauncy Gdns BLDK SG7 15 E4
Chauncy Rd STVG SG1 3 F2
Chells Enterprise Village
STVGE * SG2 36 B3
Chells La STVGE SG2 36 B1
Chells Wy STVGE SG2 36 A2
Chennells Cl HTCHE/RSTV SG4 24 A1
Chepstow Cl STVG SG1 36 A1
Chequers Bridge Rd STVG SG1 2 A2
Chequers Cl HTCH/STOT SG5 7 E4
Cherry Cl KNEB SG3 43 G3
Cherry Tree Dr STVG * SG1 2 C7
Cherry Tree Ri STVGE SG2 33 G5
Cherry Trees HNLW SG16 10 C2
Chertsey Ri STVGE SG2 36 B5
Cherwell Dr STVG SG1 31 H3
Chester Rd STVG SG1 31 H5
Chestnut Av HNLW SG16 10 C2
Chestnut Ct HTCH/STOT SG5 23 E3
Chestnut Farm HNLW SG16 5 E1
The Chestnuts WLYN AL6 42 A5
Chestnut Wk HTCHE/RSTV SG4 28 D2
STVG SG1 31 E5
Chiltern Pl HNLW SG16 4 D1
Chiltern Rd BLDK SG7 20 C2
HTCHE/RSTV SG4 23 H4
The Chilterns HTCHE/RSTV SG4 23 H5
Chiltern Vw LWTH SG6 18 C3
Chilvers Bank BLDK SG7 20 B1
Chouler Gdns STVG SG1 31 E4
Christie Rd STVGE SG2 36 B4
Church Cl WLYN AL6 42 A5
Church End ARL/CHE SG15 5 H3
STVGE SG2 33 H4
Church La ARL/CHE SG15 5 H2
HTCHE/RSTV SG4 27 G2
HTCHE/RSTV SG4 30 D2
LWTH SG6 13 H4
STVG SG1 34 D2
Church Pth HTCHE/RSTV SG4 30 A3
Church Rd HTCH/STOT SG5 7 E4
Church St BLDK SG7 14 B5
Clare Crs BLDK SG7 20 B2
Claymore Dr HTCH/STOT SG5 17 G3
Claymores STVG SG1 2 E2
Cleviscroft STVG SG1 3 F5
Clifton Pk SHFD * SG17 4 B1

Clifton Rd *HNLW* SG16 4 D1
Cloister Lawns *LWTH* SG6 19 E4
Cloisters Rd *LWTH* SG6 19 E4
The Cloisters *HTCH/STOT* * SG5 23 H3
The Close *BLDK* SG7 20 B1
STVG * SG1 30 D5
Clothall Rd *BLDK* SG7 14 C5
Clovelly Wy *STVG* SG1 34 B2
Cluny Wy *ARL/CHE* SG15 5 H5
Coach Dr *HTCHE/RSTV* SG4 28 C1
Coachman's La *BLDK* SG7 14 A5
Coach Rd *HNLW* SG16 5 E1
Coleridge Cl *HTCHE/RSTV* SG4 24 A3
Colestrete *STVG* SG1 3 H5
Colestrete Cl *STVG* SG1 3 H4
College Rd *HTCH/STOT* SG5 23 G3
Collenswood Rd *STVGE* SG2 36 A5
Collison Cl *HTCHE/RSTV* SG4 24 B1
Colts Cnr *STVGE* SG2 36 A5
Columbus Cl *STVG* SG1 35 H2
Colwell Rd *STVGE* SG2 40 B1
Colwyn Cl *STVG* SG1 34 C1
Common Ri *HTCHE/RSTV* SG4 23 H2
Common Rd *HTCH/STOT* SG5 6 D2
Common Vw *LWTH* SG6 13 F5
Conifer Wk *STVGE* SG2 36 B2
Conquest Cl *HTCHE/RSTV* SG4 28 C1
Constantine Cl *STVG* SG1 31 G5
Constantine Pl *BLDK* SG7 15 E4
Convent Cl *HTCH/STOT* SG5 23 G3
Cook Rd *STVGE* SG2 36 A2
Cooks Wy *HTCHE/RSTV* SG4 23 H2
Coopers Cl *STVGE* SG2 36 C5
The Coppens *HTCH/STOT* SG5 7 F5
Coppice Md *HTCH/STOT* SG5 6 D5
The Copse *BLDK* * SG7 20 C1
Coreys Mill La *STVG* SG1 30 C5
Cornfields *STVGE* SG2 36 B2
Corton Cl *STVG* SG1 34 C1
Cotney Cft *STVGE* SG2 40 C1
Coventry Cl *STVG* SG1 32 A5
Cowslip Hl *LWTH* SG6 18 D1
Cox's Wy *ARL/CHE* SG15 5 H5
Crabbs Cl *HTCH/STOT* * SG5 23 F4
Crabtree Dell *LWTH* SG6 19 H5
Crab Tree Rd *KNEB* SG3 43 G4
Cragside *STVGE* SG2 40 B5
Cranborne Av *HTCH/STOT* SG5 23 E5
Creamery Ct *LWTH* SG6 19 H5
The Crescent *HNLW* SG16 10 C1
HTCH/STOT SG5 23 E2
HTCHE/RSTV SG4 28 D3
LWTH SG6 19 F3
Cricketer's Rd *ARL/CHE* SG15 5 H5
Crispin Ter *HTCH/STOT* * SG5 23 E4
Croft La *LWTH* SG6 13 F4
The Crofts *HTCH/STOT* SG5 7 E4
Crompton Rd *STVG* SG1 34 B3
Cromwell Gn *LWTH* SG6 13 G5
Cromwell Rd *LWTH* SG6 13 G5
STVGE SG2 36 B4
Crossgates *STVG* SG1 3 F3
Crossleys *LWTH* SG6 13 E3
Cross St *LWTH* SG6 19 E1
Crossways Cl *HNLW* SG16 5 E1
Crow Furlong *HTCH/STOT* SG5 23 E5
Cubitt Cl *HTCHE/RSTV* SG4 24 B4
Curlew Cl *LWTH* SG6 12 D4
Cuttys La *STVG* SG1 2 E4

D

Dacre Rd *HTCH/STOT* SG5 23 H3
Dagnalls *LWTH* SG6 25 E1
Dale Cl *HTCHE/RSTV* SG4 28 C2
The Dale *LWTH* SG6 18 D2
Daltry Cl *STVG* SG1 30 D4
Daltry Rd *STVG* SG1 30 D4
Damask Cl *HTCHE/RSTV* SG4 27 E3
Damask Green Rd
HTCHE/RSTV SG4 27 E3
Dancote *KNEB* SG3 43 G2
Dane Cl *HTCH/STOT* SG5 7 E2
Dane End La *HTCHE/RSTV* SG4 32 D1
Danescroft *LWTH* SG6 13 E4
Danesgate *STVG* SG1 2 C5
Dane St *STVG* SG1 2 C4
Darby Dr *WLYN* AL6 43 F4
Darwin Rd *STVGE* SG2 36 A3
David Evans Ct *LWTH* SG6 18 C1
Davis' Rw *ARL/CHE* SG15 11 H1
Dawlish Cl *STVGE* SG2 40 B5
Dawson Cl *HNLW* SG16 4 D5
Deacons Wy *HTCH/STOT* SG5 23 E2
Deanscroft *KNEB* SG3 43 G2
Deard's End La *KNEB* SG3 43 G1
Deards Wd *KNEB* SG3 43 G2
Deeping Cl *KNEB* SG3 43 G3
The Dell *BLDK* SG7 20 B2
STVG SG1 3 F3
Denby *LWTH* SG6 19 G4
Dene La *STVGE* SG2 40 D2
Denton Rd *STVG* SG1 3 F6
Dents Cl *LWTH* SG6 19 H5
Derby Wy *STVG* SG1 36 A1
Derwent Rd *HNLW* SG16 10 C1
Desborough Rd
HTCHE/RSTV SG4 24 B3
Devonshire Cl *STVGE* SG2 39 H4
Dewpond Cl *STVG* SG1 34 D1
Ditchmore La *STVG* SG1 2 B2
Doncaster Cl *STVG* SG1 36 B1
Douglas Dr *STVG* SG1 35 H1
Dovedale *STVGE* SG2 36 A5
Downlands *BLDK* SG7 14 D4
STVGE SG2 36 C2
Drakes Dr *STVGE* SG2 36 A2
Drapers Wy *STVG* SG1 34 D2
Driver's End La *HTCHE/RSTV* SG4 42 A3
Dryden Crs *STVGE* SG2 36 B1
Duke's La *HTCH/STOT* SG5 23 F3
Duncots Cl *HTCH/STOT* SG5 17 F5
Dunhams Ct *LWTH* * SG6 19 G2
Dunhams La *LWTH* SG6 19 G2
Dunlin *LWTH* SG6 12 D4
Dunn Cl *STVG* SG1 2 E7
Durham Rd *STVG* SG1 31 H5
Dyes La *HTCHE/RSTV* SG4 38 A1
Dymoke Ms *STVG* * SG1 34 D2

E

Earlsmead *LWTH* SG6 19 E5
Eastbourne Av *STVG* SG1 34 B3
Eastcheap *LWTH* SG6 19 E3
East Cl *HTCHE/RSTV* SG4 24 A2
STVG SG1 3 G3
Eastern Av *HNLW* SG16 10 D2
Eastern Wy *LWTH* SG6 13 F4
Eastgate *STVG* SG1 2 D5
Eastholm *LWTH* SG6 13 F5
Eastholm Gn *LWTH* SG6 13 F5
East Reach *STVGE* SG2 39 H2
East Vw *HTCHE/RSTV* SG4 29 F4
Edgeworth Cl *STVGE* SG2 40 B3
Edison Rd *STVGE* SG2 36 A3
Edmonds Dr *STVGE* SG2 36 C5
Eisenberg Cl *BLDK* SG7 14 D4
Elbow La *STVGE* SG2 40 A3
Eldefield *LWTH* SG6 18 C1
Elderberry Dr *HTCHE/RSTV* SG4 28 D2
Elder Wy *STVG* SG1 2 D7
Eliot Rd *STVGE* SG2 36 B3
Ellis Av *STVG* SG1 35 F1
Elm Cl *HNLW* SG16 5 E1
Elm Pk *BLDK* SG7 14 C5
Elms Cl *HTCHE/RSTV* SG4 29 H3
Elmside Wk *HTCH/STOT* SG5 23 F4
The Elms *WLYN* AL6 42 A5
Elm Wk *STVGE* SG2 40 A1
Elmwood Av *BLDK* SG7 20 C1
Elmwood Ct *BLDK* * SG7 14 C5
Ely Cl *STVG* SG1 32 A4
Emperors Ga *STVGE* SG2 36 C1
Ennismore Cl *LWTH* SG6 19 H5
Essex Rd *STVG* SG1 34 C1
Everest Cl *ARL/CHE* SG15 6 A5
Evergreen Cl *KNEB* SG3 43 H5
Exchange Rd *STVG* SG1 3 G3
Exeter Cl *STVG* SG1 32 A4
Eynsford Ct *HTCHE/RSTV* SG4 23 G5

F

Fairfield Wy *HTCHE/RSTV* SG4 24 B3
STVG SG1 32 B3
Fairlands Wy *STVG* SG1 2 A3
STVGE SG2 36 A1
Fairview Rd *STVG* SG1 34 C1
Falcon Cl *STVGE* SG2 40 C2
Fallowfield *STVGE* SG2 40 B1
Faraday Rd *STVGE* SG2 36 A3
Farm Cl *LWTH* SG6 13 F4
STVG SG1 2 E6
Farriers Cl *BLDK* SG7 14 B4
Farthing Dr *LWTH* SG6 19 H5
Fawcett Rd *STVGE* SG2 36 A1
Featherston Rd *STVGE* SG2 40 B1
Fellowes Wy *STVGE* SG2 39 G2
Fells Cl *HTCH/STOT* SG5 23 G3
Fen End *HTCH/STOT* SG5 7 E2
Ferrier Rd *STVGE* SG2 36 B3
Fieldfare *LWTH* SG6 12 D4
STVGE SG2 40 C1
Field La *LWTH* SG6 19 E4
Fifth Av *LWTH* SG6 19 H2
Filey Cl *STVG* SG1 34 B2
Finches End *STVGE* SG2 37 G1
The Finches *HTCHE/RSTV* SG4 23 H4
Fir Cl *STVGE* SG2 39 G3
Firecrest *LWTH* SG6 12 D4
Firs Cl *HTCH/STOT* SG5 23 E3
Fishers Gn *STVG* SG1 30 B5
Fisher's Green Rd *STVG* SG1 34 C1
Fishponds Rd *HTCH/STOT* SG5 23 F3
Fleetwood Crs *STVG* SG1 34 C2
Flinders Cl *STVGE* SG2 36 B4
Flint Rd *LWTH* SG6 13 H5
Florence St *HTCH/STOT* SG5 23 G3
Foldingshott *KNEB* SG3 44 C4
Folly Cl *HTCHE/RSTV* SG4 28 D1
Football Cl *BLDK* SG7 14 B4
Fore St *HTCHE/RSTV* SG4 27 E2
Forest Rw *STVGE* SG2 39 G3
Forge Cl *HTCH/STOT* SG5 23 G3
Fortuna Cl *STVGE* SG2 36 B1
The Forum *STVG* SG1 2 C3
Foster Cl *STVG* SG1 30 D5
Foster Dr *HTCHE/RSTV* SG4 28 D1
Fouracres *LWTH* SG6 25 F1
Four Acres *STVG* SG1 35 E2
Fourth Av *LWTH* SG6 19 H1
Foxfield *STVGE* SG2 40 B1
Fox Rd *STVG* SG1 2 E4
Francis Cl *HTCH/STOT* SG5 6 D4
HTCHE/RSTV SG4 28 D1
Franklin Gdns *HTCHE/RSTV* SG4 24 A2
Franklin's Rd *STVG* SG1 34 D1
Franks Cl *HNLW* SG16 4 C5
Fraser Cnr *STVGE* * SG2 36 A2
Fred Millard Ct *STVG* * SG1 3 F4
Freemans Cl *HTCH/STOT* SG5 22 D2
Freewaters Cl *HTCH/STOT* SG5 17 F4
Frensham Dr *HTCHE/RSTV* SG4 24 B1
Friars Rd *HTCHE/RSTV* SG4 27 E2
Friday Furlong *HTCH/STOT* SG5 22 D3
Frobisher Dr *STVGE* SG2 36 A2
Froghall La *STVGE* SG2 33 G5
Frogmore Hl *HERT/WAS* SG14 45 F1
Fry Rd *STVGE* SG2 36 B4
Fullers Ct *LWTH* SG6 18 D1
Fulton Cl *STVG* SG1 2 A4
Furlay Cl *LWTH* SG6 18 C1
Furzedown *STVGE* SG2 36 A5

G

Gainsford Crs *HTCHE/RSTV* SG4 24 B1
Gaping La *HTCH/STOT* SG5 23 E4
Garden Fld *STVGE* SG2 40 D2
Garden Rd *KNEB* SG3 44 A5
Garden Rw *HTCH/STOT* SG5 23 G3
The Gardens *BLDK* SG7 14 B5
HNLW SG16 5 E1
HTCH/STOT SG5 6 D4
Garden Wk *STVG* SG1 2 E4
Garth Rd *LWTH* SG6 18 D5
Gates Wy *STVG* SG1 2 B2
Gaunts Wy *LWTH* SG6 13 E3
George Leighton Ct *STVGE* SG2 36 A4
Gernon Rd *LWTH* SG6 19 E3
Gernon Wk *LWTH* SG6 19 E3
Gibbons Wy *KNEB* SG3 43 G3
Gibson Cl *HTCHE/RSTV* SG4 24 A4
Gillison Cl *LWTH* SG6 19 G3
Gipsy La *KNEB* SG3 43 F4
Girdle Rd *HTCHE/RSTV* SG4 23 H1
Girons Cl *HTCHE/RSTV* SG4 24 A4
The Glade *BLDK* SG7 20 B1
LWTH SG6 19 E5
Glebe Av *ARL/CHE* SG15 5 H3
Glebe Rd *LWTH* SG6 19 F1
The Glebe *HTCHE/RSTV* * SG4 29 F4
STVGE SG2 36 A3
Glenwood Cl *STVGE* SG2 40 B2
Gloucester Cl *STVG* SG1 31 F4
The Glynde *STVGE* SG2 40 A4
Goddard End *STVGE* SG2 40 B3
Godfrey Cl *STVGE* SG2 40 A1
Goldon *LWTH* SG6 19 G4
Gonville Crs *STVGE* SG2 40 B2
Gordian Wy *STVG* SG1 32 B5
Gorleston Cl *STVG* SG1 30 B5
Gorst Cl *LWTH* SG6 18 D3
Gosmore Ley Cl
HTCHE/RSTV SG4 28 C3
Gosmore Rd *HTCHE/RSTV* SG4 28
Gothic Wy *ARL/CHE* SG15 5
Grace Wy *STVG* SG1 3
Grammar School Wk
HTCH/STOT SG5 23
Granby Rd *STVG* SG1 30
Grange Cl *HTCHE/RSTV* SG4 28
Grange Ct *LWTH* * SG6 13
Grange Dr *HTCH/STOT* SG5 7
Grange Rd *LWTH* SG6 13
Granville Rd *HTCHE/RSTV* SG4 24
Grasmere *STVG* SG1 32
Grass Mdw *STVGE* SG2 36
Graveley La *HTCHE/RSTV* SG4 30
Graveley Rd *HTCHE/RSTV* SG4 24
STVG SG1 30
Gray's La *HTCH/STOT* SG5 23
Great Ashby Wy *STVG* SG1 31
Great Lawne *KNEB* SG3 44
Great North Rd *STVG* SG1 39
Green Acres *STVGE* SG2 40
Green Cl *STVGE* SG2 39
Greenfield Av *HTCH/STOT* SG5 17
Greenfield La *HTCH/STOT* SG5 17
Greenfield Rd *STVG* SG1 35
Green La *HTCHE/RSTV* SG4 24
LWTH SG6 13
Greenside Dr *HTCH/STOT* SG5 23
Green St *STVG* SG1 34
The Green *HTCH/STOT* SG5 7
KNEB SG3 42
Greenway *LWTH* SG6 25
STVGE SG2 37
Greenways *STVG* SG1 2
Grenville Wy *STVGE* SG2 39
Gresley Wy *STVGE* SG2 36
Greydells Rd *STVG* SG1 2
Grimstone Rd *HTCHE/RSTV* SG4 29
Grinders End *HTCHE/RSTV* SG4 30
Grosvenor Rd *BLDK* SG7 14
Grosvenor Rd West *BLDK* SG7 14
Grovelands Av *HTCHE/RSTV* SG4 24
Groveland Wy *HTCH/STOT* SG5 7
Grove Rd *HTCH/STOT* SG5 23
STVG SG1 34
Guildford Cl *STVG* SG1 31
Gun La *KNEB* SG3 43
Gun Meadow Av *KNEB* SG3 43
Gunnels Wood Pk *STVG* * SG1 2
Gunnels Wood Rd *STVG* SG1 2
Gun Rd *KNEB* SG3 43
Gun Road Gdns *KNEB* SG3 43
Gurney's La *HTCH/STOT* SG5 16

H

Haddon Cl *STVGE* SG2 40
Hadrians Wk *STVGE* SG2 36
Hadrian Wy *LWTH* SG6 20
Hadwell Cl *STVGE* SG2 3
Half Acre *HTCH/STOT* SG5 23
Hall La *KNEB* SG3 43
Hall Md *LWTH* SG6 18
Hallworth Dr *HTCH/STOT* SG5 6
Halsey Dr *HTCHE/RSTV* SG4 24
Hammond Cl *STVG* SG1 2
Hampden Cl *LWTH* SG6 13
Hampden Rd *HTCHE/RSTV* SG4 24
Hampton Cl *STVGE* SG2 40
Hanover Cl *STVGE* SG2 39
Hardwick Cl *STVGE* SG2 40
Hardy Cl *HTCHE/RSTV* SG4 24
Harefield *STVGE* SG2 40
Harkness Wy *HTCHE/RSTV* SG4 24
Harper Ct *STVG* * SG1 3
Harrison Cl *HTCHE/RSTV* SG4 23
Harrow Ct *STVG* SG1 2
Harrowdene *STVGE* SG2 36
Harvest Ct *LWTH* * SG6 19
Harvest La *STVGE* SG2 3
Harvey Rd *STVGE* SG2 3
Haselfoot *LWTH* SG6 1
Hastings Cl *STVG* SG1 3
Hatch La *BLDK* SG7 2
Hawkins Hall La *KNEB* SG3 4
Hawthorn Cl *HTCH/STOT* SG5 2
Hawthorn Hl *LWTH* SG6 1
The Hawthorns *STVG* SG1
Haycroft Rd *STVG* SG1 3
Hayfield *STVGE* SG2 3
Haygarth *KNEB* SG3 4
Hayley Common *STVGE* SG2 3
Haymoor *LWTH* SG6 1
Haysman Cl *LWTH* SG6 1
Hazel Gv *HTCH/STOT* SG5
Hazelmere Rd *STVGE* SG2 3

zelwood Cl HTCH/STOT SG5 23 G3
adingley Cl STVG SG1 35 F1
athermere LWTH SG6 13 E4
athfield Rd HTCH/STOT SG5 23 G1
dgerow Cl STVGE SG2 36 C2
e Hedgerows STVGE SG2 36 C1
llards Rd STVG SG1 35 E2
nsley Cl HTCHE/RSTV SG4 24 A5
rmitage Rd HTCH/STOT SG5 23 G4
rne Rd STVG SG1 30 C5
ron Wy HTCH/STOT SG5 6 D4
rtford Rd STVGE SG2 39 G4
rtfordshire Wy
HTCHE/RSTV SG4 25 G4
ggins Wk STVG SG1 30 D5
ggin Wk STVG * SG1 31 F5
gh Av LWTH SG6 18 C3
ghbury Rd HTCHE/RSTV SG4 23 H4
ghbush Rd HTCH/STOT SG5 6 D5
gh Dane HTCHE/RSTV SG4 23 H1
ghfield LWTH SG6 18 C4
ghfield Ct STVG SG1 35 F2
ghover Rd LWTH SG6 18 C3
ghover Wy HTCHE/RSTV SG4 24 A2
gh Plash STVG * SG1 2 E4
gh St ARL/CHE SG15 5 H4
BLDK SG7 14 C5
HTCH/STOT SG5 7 E4
HTCH/STOT SG5 23 F4
HTCHE/RSTV SG4 28 C3
HTCHE/RSTV SG4 30 D2
STVG SG1 34 D2
STVGE SG2 33 G5
STVGE SG2 37 G1
gh Vw HTCH/STOT SG5 23 E5
ary Ri ARL/CHE SG15 6 A5
brow LWTH SG6 18 C3
crest BLDK SG7 20 C1
STVG SG1 3 F3
crest Pk LWTH * SG6 18 B2
field Av HTCHE/RSTV SG4 23 H1
gate HTCHE/RSTV SG4 17 H5
mead STVG SG1 3 J2
shott LWTH SG6 19 F2
side STVG SG1 3 H3
side Pk BLDK * SG7 20 D1
Top BLDK SG7 20 B1
ton Cl STVG SG1 34 C2
e Wy HTCH/STOT SG5 22 D2
chin Hl HTCHE/RSTV SG4 23 F5
chin La SHFD SG17 4 C1
chin Rd ARL/CHE SG15 11 H2
TCH/STOT SG5 12 C2
TCH/STOT SG5 22 A3
TCHE/RSTV SG4 24 C5
TCHE/RSTV SG4 27 E2
TCHE/RSTV SG4 28 C2
WTH SG6 18 D5
HFD SG17 4 A3
TVG SG1 30 C4
chin St BLDK SG7 14 B5
dbrook HTCHE/RSTV SG4 24 A4
den Cl HTCHE/RSTV SG4 24 B4
ders La STVGE SG2 36 D4
low La HTCHE/RSTV SG4 23 G4
lybush La KNEB SG3 44 B4
ly Copse STVG SG1 3 G5
ly Leys STVGE SG2 40 A4
ly Shaws STVGE SG2 40 A2
mdale LWTH SG6 19 F3
royd Crs BLDK SG7 20 B1
well Rd HTCH/STOT SG5 16 A2
ne Cl HTCH/STOT SG5 7 E4
nefield La HTCHE/RSTV SG4 38 A2
nestead Moat STVG SG1 3 F4
ewell Rd BLDK SG7 14 A5
ton Rd STVG SG1 34 B2
ace Gay Gdns LWTH SG6 18 D3
nbeam Spring KNEB SG3 43 G3
Hornbeams STVGE SG2 36 A5
pital Rd ARL/CHE SG15 11 G2
se La ARL/CHE SG15 5 H3
vard Cl HTCH/STOT * SG5 6 D5
vard Dr LWTH SG6 19 G5
vard Ga LWTH SG6 19 G4
vards Wd LWTH SG6 19 G5
son Rd STVGE SG2 36 A2
ters Cl HTCH/STOT SG5 6 D4
TVGE SG2 36 C2
tingdon Rd STVG SG1 34 C1
ting Ga HTCHE/RSTV SG4 17 H5
st Cl BLDK SG7 14 D4
ean Wy STVGE SG2 39 H1
e Av HTCH/STOT SG5 6 D5
e Gn STVGE SG2 40 A1
e Gn East STVGE SG2 40 A1
e Gn North STVGE SG2 40 A1
e Gn South STVGE SG2 40 A1
The Hyde STVGE SG2 40 B1

I

Ibberson Wy HTCHE/RSTV SG4 23 H4
Iceni Ct LWTH SG6 19 G1
Ickleford Rd HTCH/STOT SG5 23 G3
Icknield Cl HTCH/STOT SG5 17 F4
Icknield Gn LWTH SG6 18 D2
Icknield Wy BLDK SG7 14 B4
LWTH SG6 18 B2
Icknield Wy East BLDK SG7 14 C4
Icknield Way Pth BLDK SG7 14 B2
HTCH/STOT SG5 17 G3
The Icon STVG * SG1 2 D4
Ingelheim Ct STVG SG1 35 E2
Ingleside Dr STVG SG1 30 C5
Inn's Cl STVG SG1 2 C1
Inskip Crs STVG SG1 3 F3
Iona Cl STVG SG1 31 G4
Iredale Vw BLDK SG7 14 D4
Islington Wy STVG SG1 31 G4
Ivel Rd STVG SG1 34 D2
Ivel Wy BLDK SG7 20 D2
HTCH/STOT SG5 7 E2

J

Jackdaw Cl STVGE SG2 36 C5
Jackman's Pl LWTH SG6 19 G2
Jacks Hill Pk HTCHE/RSTV * SG4 25 H5
Jackson St BLDK SG7 14 B4
James Wy STVG SG1 34 D2
Jarden LWTH SG6 19 H4
Jay Cl LWTH SG6 12 D5
Jennings Cl STVG SG1 2 E7
Jessop Rd STVG SG1 31 H5
Jeve Cl BLDK SG7 14 D4
Jill Grey Pl HTCH/STOT SG5 23 G5
John Barker Pl HTCH/STOT SG5 22 D2
John Howland Cl HNLW SG16 5 E2
Jubilee Crs ARL/CHE SG15 11 G3
Jubilee Rd LWTH SG6 19 H1
STVG SG1 34 C1
Julia Ga STVG SG1 36 B1
Julian's Ct STVG SG1 34 D1
Julian's Rd STVG SG1 34 C1
Jupiter Ga STVGE SG2 36 C1

K

Kardwell Cl HTCHE/RSTV SG4 23 H5
Keats Cl STVGE SG2 36 A1
Keats Wy HTCHE/RSTV SG4 24 B4
Keiths Wd KNEB SG3 43 G2
Keller Cl STVGE SG2 36 A5
Kendale Rd HTCHE/RSTV SG4 23 G5
Kenilworth Cl STVGE SG2 40 B5
Kenmare Cl STVG SG1 35 E2
Kent Pl HTCH/STOT * SG5 23 E3
Kerr Cl KNEB SG3 43 G2
Kershaw's Hl HTCHE/RSTV SG4 23 G5
Kessingland Av STVG SG1 30 B5
Kestrel Cl STVGE SG2 40 C2
Kestrel Wk LWTH SG6 19 G5
Kimberley LWTH SG6 13 E3
Kimbolton Crs KNEB SG3 39 H4
Kingfisher Ct HTCHE/RSTV SG4 23 H5
Kingfisher Ri STVGE SG2 40 C2
King George Cl STVG SG1 2 E2
King Georges Cl HTCH/STOT SG5 23 E1
Kingsdown HTCHE/RSTV SG4 24 A4
King's Rd HTCH/STOT SG5 23 G3
STVG SG1 2 C6
Kings Walden Ri STVGE SG2 36 B2
Kingsway HTCH/STOT SG5 6 D3
Kings Wy STVG SG1 2 A5
Kingswood Av HTCHE/RSTV SG4 24 C3
Kipling Cl HTCHE/RSTV SG4 24 B4
Kitcheners La STVGE SG2 33 G5
Kitching La STVG SG1 34 A4
Kite Wy LWTH SG6 12 D5
Knap Cl LWTH SG6 13 H5
Knights Templars Gn STVGE SG2 36 B1
Knowl Piece HTCHE/RSTV SG4 17 H5
Kristiansand Wy LWTH SG6 13 H5
Kymswell Rd STVGE SG2 36 B5
Kyrkeby LWTH SG6 19 H4

L

Lacre Wy LWTH SG6 19 H1
Lamb Meadow ARL/CHE SG15 11 G2
Lammas Md HTCH/STOT SG5 23 F1
Lammas Pth STVGE SG2 36 A5
Lammas Wy LWTH SG6 13 E5
Lancaster Cl STVG SG1 31 F4
Lancaster Rd HTCH/STOT SG5 23 F3
Langbridge Cl HTCHE/RSTV SG4 28 D1
Langleigh LWTH * SG6 13 E4
Langley Sidings STVG * SG1 39 F2
Langthorne Av STVG SG1 2 E1
Lannock LWTH SG6 19 H4
Lannock Hl HTCHE/RSTV SG4 26 A1
Lanterns La STVGE SG2 36 C3
Lapwing Dell LWTH SG6 25 G1
Lapwing Ri STVGE SG2 40 C2
Larch Av HTCHE/RSTV SG4 28 D2
Larkins Cl BLDK SG7 14 C4
Larkinson STVG SG1 34 D2
Larwood Gv STVG SG1 35 H1
Latchmore Cl HTCHE/RSTV SG4 28 C1
Laurel Wy HTCH/STOT SG5 17 F5
Lavender Ct BLDK SG7 14 B4
Lavender Wy HTCH/STOT SG5 23 E4
The Lawns STVGE SG2 36 C5
Lawrence Av LWTH SG6 19 F4
STVG SG1 35 F2
Lawrence Md HTCHE/RSTV * SG4 30 A2
Laxton Gdns BLDK SG7 20 D1
The Leas BLDK SG7 20 B1
Leaves Spring STVGE SG2 39 G2
Leggett Gv STVG SG1 35 F1
Leslie Cl STVGE SG2 40 B2
Letchmore Cl STVG SG1 2 C1
Letchmore Rd STVG SG1 2 B1
Letchworth Ga LWTH SG6 19 G5
Letchworth La LWTH SG6 19 E5
Letchworth Point LWTH * SG6 19 G2
Letchworth Rd BLDK SG7 20 A1
Lewis La ARL/CHE SG15 5 H4
Leyden Rd STVG SG1 39 E1
Leys Av LWTH SG6 19 E2
Lime Cl STVGE SG2 36 C5
Limekiln La BLDK SG7 20 C1
The Limes ARL/CHE SG15 5 H2
HTCH/STOT SG5 23 E5
Lincoln Rd STVG SG1 32 A4
Lindencroft LWTH SG6 13 F4
The Lindens STVG SG1 3 F5
Lindsay Av HTCHE/RSTV SG4 29 E1
Lingfield Rd STVG SG1 32 B5
Linkways East STVG SG1 3 G3
Linkways West STVG SG1 3 G3
Linnet Cl LWTH SG6 12 D5
Linten Cl HTCHE/RSTV SG4 24 B5
Lintott Cl STVG SG1 2 C1
Lismore STVGE SG2 40 B3
Lister Av HTCHE/RSTV SG4 28 C1
Lister Cl STVG SG1 30 D4
Littlebury Cl HTCH/STOT SG5 7 F5
Little Hyde STVGE SG2 36 A5
Livingstone Link STVGE SG2 36 A1
Lodge Ct HTCH/STOT SG5 17 F5
Lodge Wy STVGE SG2 39 H3
Lomond Wy STVG SG1 32 B4
London Rd BLDK SG7 20 C2
HTCHE/RSTV SG4 28 C1
KNEB SG3 43 H4
STVG SG1 2 D7
London Rw ARL/CHE SG15 11 H2
Long Cl HNLW * SG16 10 A2
Longcroft Rd STVG SG1 35 F2
Longfields STVGE SG2 40 B3
Long Hyde STVGE SG2 36 A5
Long La STVGE SG2 36 D4
Long Leaves STVGE SG2 39 H2
Longmead KNEB SG3 43 H5
LWTH SG6 18 D1
Longmeadow Dr
HTCH/STOT SG5 17 F3
Long Rdg STVGE SG2 40 C3
Lonsdale Ct STVG SG1 35 G2
Lonsdale Rd STVG SG1 3 G1
Lordship La LWTH SG6 19 G4
Lovell Cl HTCHE/RSTV SG4 23 H5
Lower Innings HTCH/STOT SG5 22 D3
Lower Sean STVGE SG2 39 H1
Lowes Cl STVG SG1 32 B4
Lucas La HTCH/STOT SG5 23 E4
Lygrave STVGE SG2 40 B4
Lyle's Rw HTCHE/RSTV SG4 23 G5
Lymans Rd ARL/CHE SG15 5 H4
Lymington Rd STVG SG1 34 C1
Lyndale STVG SG1 2 E5
Lynton Av ARL/CHE SG15 5 H5
Lytton Av LWTH SG6 19 E3
Lytton Flds KNEB SG3 43 G2
Lytton Wy STVG SG1 2 B4

M

Mackenzie Sq STVGE SG2 40 A1
Maddles LWTH SG6 20 A4
Made Feld STVG SG1 3 G3
Magellan Cl STVGE SG2 36 C4
Magpie Crs STVGE SG2 36 C5
Maiden St HTCHE/RSTV SG4 27 F2
Mallard Rd STVGE SG2 40 C2
Malthouse La HTCH/STOT SG5 7 F3
Maltings Cl BLDK SG7 14 D4
The Maltings Norton Hall Farm
LWTH * SG6 13 H4
The Maltings HNLW * SG16 5 E1
STVGE SG2 37 G1
Manchester Cl STVG SG1 31 G3
Mandeville STVGE SG2 40 B3
Manley Hwy HTCH/STOT SG5 22 C4
Manor Cl HTCH/STOT SG5 17 F5
LWTH SG6 19 E5
Manor Crs HTCHE/RSTV SG4 24 A5
Manor Rd HNLW SG16 4 D1
Manor Vw STVGE SG2 40 A3
Manor Wy KNEB SG3 42 D2
LWTH SG6 19 E5
Mansfield Rd BLDK SG7 20 B1
Manton Rd HTCHE/RSTV SG4 24 B5
The Maples HTCHE/RSTV SG4 28 C1
STVGE * SG2 40 A4
Mardleybury Ct KNEB * SG3 43 H5
Market Pl STVG SG1 2 D4
Market Sq STVG SG1 2 D4
Marlborough Cl
HTCHE/RSTV SG4 27 E3
Marlborough Rd STVGE SG2 36 B4
Marlowe Cl STVGE SG2 36 B1
Marmet Av LWTH SG6 18 D2
Marschefield HTCH/STOT SG5 6 D4
Marshgate STVG SG1 2 D3
Martins Wy STVG SG1 34 D1
Martin Wy LWTH SG6 18 C3
Marymead Ct STVGE SG2 39 H4
Marymead Dr STVGE SG2 39 H4
Masefield HTCHE/RSTV SG4 24 B4
Mathews Cl STVG SG1 31 E5
Matthew Ga HTCHE/RSTV SG4 28 D1
Mattocke Rd HTCH/STOT SG5 22 D2
Maxwell Rd STVG SG1 34 C4
Maycroft LWTH SG6 13 F4
Maydencroft La HTCH/STOT SG5 28 A2
Mayles Cl STVG SG1 34 C2
Maylin Cl HTCHE/RSTV SG4 24 B3
Mayshades Cl KNEB SG3 43 H5
Maytrees HTCHE/RSTV SG4 23 H5
Mead Cl STVG SG1 3 H2
Meadowbank HTCHE/RSTV SG4 24 A2
Meadow Cl KNEB SG3 44 C5
Meadowsweet HNLW SG16 10 A3
Meadow Wy HTCH/STOT SG5 6 D4
HTCH/STOT SG5 23 E5
LWTH SG6 19 E3
STVG SG1 3 H3
Meads Ctyd STVGE * SG2 36 B2
The Meads LWTH SG6 18 D2
The Mead HTCH/STOT SG5 23 F1
Meadway KNEB SG3 43 G3
STVG SG1 34 B3
Medalls Link STVGE SG2 3 K7
Medalls Pth STVGE SG2 3 K7
Meeting House La BLDK SG7 14 B4
Melbourn Cl HTCH/STOT SG5 7 E5
Melne Rd STVGE SG2 40 A4
Melvern Cl STVGE SG2 40 A5
Merchants Wk BLDK SG7 15 E4
Mercia Rd BLDK SG7 14 D5
Meredith Rd STVG SG1 35 H2
Mermaid Cl HTCHE/RSTV SG4 24 A4
The Mews Norton Hall Farm
LWTH * SG6 13 H4
Middlefields LWTH SG6 13 E5
Middlefields Ct LWTH * SG6 13 E4
Middle Rw STVG SG1 34 D2
Middlesborough Cl STVG SG1 31 G4
Midhurst LWTH SG6 12 D5
Mildmay Rd STVG SG1 36 A1
Milestone Cl STVGE SG2 36 C5
Milestone Rd HTCH/STOT SG5 23 E2
KNEB SG3 43 H2
Milksey La HTCHE/RSTV SG4 30 C1
Millard Wy HTCHE/RSTV SG4 24 B1
Mill Cl HTCH/STOT SG5 7 F4

Millfield La *HTCHE/RSTV* SG4 28 C2
Mill La *ARL/CHE* SG15 11 G1
HTCH/STOT SG5 7 F4
HTCH/STOT SG5 7 E1
HTCHE/RSTV SG4 27 F2
HTCHE/RSTV SG4 28 C3
Mill Rd *HTCHE/RSTV* SG4 28 C3
Millstream Cl *HTCHE/RSTV* SG4 23 H1
Milne Cl *LWTH* SG6 19 G5
Milton Vw *HTCHE/RSTV* SG4 24 B4
Minehead Wy *STVG* SG1 34 B2
Minerva Cl *STVG* SG1 32 B5
Minsden Rd *STVGE* SG2 40 C1
The Mixies *HTCH/STOT* SG5 6 D4
Mobbsbury Wy *STVGE* SG2 36 A2
Monklands *LWTH* SG6 18 C2
Monks Cl *LWTH* SG6 18 B2
Monks Vw *STVGE* SG2 39 G2
Monkswood Wy *STVG* SG1 2 E6
STVGE SG2 39 F2
Mons Av *BLDK* SG7 20 C2
Montfitchet Wk *STVGE* SG2 36 C2
Moorhead Cl *HTCH/STOT* SG5 23 E5
Moormead Hl *HTCH/STOT* SG5 22 D5
Moors Ley *STVGE* SG2 33 F5
Morecambe Cl *STVG* SG1 34 C2
Morgan Cl *STVG* SG1 31 E5
Morris Cl *HNLW* SG16 4 D5
Moss Wy *HTCH/STOT* SG5 22 D2
Motts Cl *HERT/WAS* SG14 45 H3
Mount Garrison
HTCHE/RSTV SG4 23 G4
Mountjoy *HTCHE/RSTV* SG4 24 B2
Mount Pleasant *HTCH/STOT* SG5 23 E5
Mowbray Crs *HTCH/STOT* SG5 7 E4
Mowbray Gdns
HTCHE/RSTV SG4 28 D1
Mozart Ct *STVG* SG1 2 A3
Muddy La *LWTH* SG6 19 E5
Muirhead Wy *KNEB* SG3 43 G2
Mulberry Wy *HTCH/STOT* SG5 23 E1
Mullway *LWTH* SG6 18 B2
Mundesley Cl *STVG* SG1 30 C5
The Muntings *STVGE* SG2 3 J7
Munts Meadow
HTCHE/RSTV SG4 27 F2
Murrell La *HTCH/STOT* SG5 7 F5

N

Nash Cl *STVGE* SG2 36 A3
Neagh Cl *STVG* SG1 32 B3
Nene Rd *HNLW* SG16 10 C1
Neptune Ga *STVGE* SG2 32 C5
Netherstones *HTCH/STOT* SG5 7 E3
Netley Dell *LWTH* SG6 19 G5
Nevell's Gn *LWTH* SG6 19 E1
Nevells Rd *LWTH* SG6 19 E2
Nevilles Ct *LWTH* * SG6 19 G1
Newbury Cl *STVG* SG1 31 E5
Newcastle Cl *STVG* SG1 31 G4
New Cl *KNEB* SG3 43 G1
New Ct *KNEB* * SG3 43 H5
Newells *LWTH* SG6 20 A4
New England Cl
HTCHE/RSTV SG4 28 C2
Newgate *STVGE* SG2 3 K7
Newlands *LWTH* SG6 19 F5
Newlands Cl East
HTCHE/RSTV SG4 28 C2
Newlands Cl West
HTCHE/RSTV SG4 28 C2
Newlands La *HTCHE/RSTV* SG4 28 C2
Newlyn Cl *STVG* SG1 34 B3
Newnham Rd *BLDK* SG7 8 A5
Newnham Wy *BLDK* SG7 8 D1
New Park La *STVGE* SG2 40 D2
New Rd *KNEB* SG3 44 A4
SHFD SG17 4 B1
Newton Rd *STVGE* SG2 36 A3
Newtons Wy *HTCHE/RSTV* SG4 23 G5
Nicholas Pl *STVG* SG1 31 E5
Nightingale Rd *HTCH/STOT* SG5 23 G3
Nightingale Wk *STVGE* SG2 36 B4
Nightingale Wy *BLDK* SG7 20 B2
Nimbus Wy *HTCHE/RSTV* SG4 24 B4
Ninesprings Wy
HTCHE/RSTV SG4 24 B5
Ninning's La *WLYN* AL6 43 E5
Nodes Dr *STVGE* SG2 39 H3
Nokeside *STVGE* SG2 40 A4
The Noke *STVGE* SG2 40 A4
Normans Cl *LWTH* SG6 13 E4
Normans La *WLYN* AL6 43 F5
North Av *LWTH* SG6 13 G5
Northern Av *HNLW* SG16 10 C2
Northfields *LWTH* SG6 13 E4
North Rd *BLDK* SG7 14 B3
STVG SG1 30 D4
Norton Bury La *LWTH* SG6 13 H3
Norton Crs *BLDK* SG7 14 B5
Norton Gn *STVG* * SG1 38 C1
Norton Green Rd *STVG* SG1 2 B7
Norton Mill La *LWTH* SG6 14 A2
Norton Rd *HTCH/STOT* SG5 7 F5
LWTH SG6 13 F5
STVG SG1 2 B6
Norton Wy North *LWTH* SG6 13 F5
Norton Wy South *LWTH* SG6 19 F2
Norwich Cl *STVG* SG1 32 A5
Nun's Cl *HTCH/STOT* SG5 23 F4
Nursery Cl *STVGE* SG2 39 H4
Nutcroft *KNEB* SG3 44 C5
Nutleigh Gv *HTCH/STOT* SG5 23 E2

O

Oak Dr *HNLW* SG16 5 E1
Oakfield Av *HTCHE/RSTV* SG4 29 E1
Oakfields *STVGE* SG2 40 A3
Oakfields Av *KNEB* SG3 43 H1
Oakfields Cl *STVGE* SG2 40 B3
Oakfields Rd *KNEB* SG3 43 H1
Oakhill *LWTH* SG6 20 A4
Oak La *HTCHE/RSTV* SG4 30 C2
Oaks Cl *HTCHE/RSTV* SG4 28 C1
Oaks Cross *STVGE* SG2 40 A4
Oak Tree Cl *LWTH* SG6 18 D4
Oakwell Cl *STVGE* SG2 40 C5
Oakwood Cl *STVGE* SG2 40 B2
Offley Rd *HTCH/STOT* SG5 23 E5
Old Bourne Wy *STVG* SG1 31 H3
Old Brewery Cl *HTCH/STOT* SG5 7 E3
Old Chantry La *STVG* SG1 30 B4
Old Charlton Rd *HTCH/STOT* SG5 23 F5
Olden Md *LWTH* SG6 19 G5
Olde Swann Ct *STVG* SG1 34 D1
Oldfield Farm Rd *HNLW* SG16 10 C1
Old Hale Wy *HTCH/STOT* SG5 23 F2
Old Knebworth La *KNEB* SG3 42 D1
Old La *KNEB* SG3 44 A2
Old Oak Cl *ARL/CHE* SG15 5 H2
Old Park Rd *HTCH/STOT* SG5 23 F4
Old School Wk *ARL/CHE* SG15 11 H1
The Old Walled Gdn *STVG* SG1 30 D5
Oliver's La *HTCH/STOT* SG5 7 E3
Olympus Rd *HNLW* SG16 10 C1
Openshaw Wy *LWTH* SG6 19 F2
Orchard Cl *HTCHE/RSTV* SG4 28 C3
LWTH SG6 13 E5
Orchard Crs *STVG* SG1 34 D2
Orchard Rd *BLDK* SG7 14 B5
HTCHE/RSTV SG4 24 A2
STVG SG1 34 C1
The Orchard *BLDK* SG7 14 C5
Orchard Wy *HNLW* SG16 10 B2
KNEB SG3 43 F2
LWTH SG6 13 E5
Ordelmere *LWTH* SG6 13 E4
Orlando Cl *HTCHE/RSTV* SG4 23 H5
Orwell Vw *BLDK* SG7 15 E4
Osprey Gdns *STVGE* SG2 40 C2
Osterley Cl *STVGE* SG2 40 B5
Oughtonhead La
HTCH/STOT SG5 22 C3
Oughton Head Wy
HTCH/STOT SG5 23 E3
Oundle Ct *STVGE* SG2 40 B4
Oundle Pth *STVGE* SG2 40 B4
The Oundle *STVGE* SG2 40 B3
The Oval *HNLW* SG16 10 D2
Owen Jones Cl *HNLW* SG16 4 D5
Oxleys Rd *STVGE* SG2 40 A1

P

Pacatian Wy *STVGE* SG2 36 B1
Paddock Cl *LWTH* SG6 19 E3
Paddocks Cl *STVGE* SG2 40 A1
The Paddocks *STVGE* SG2 40 A1
The Paddock *HTCHE/RSTV* SG4 28 D1
Page Cl *BLDK* SG7 20 C2
Pankhurst Crs *STVGE* SG2 36 B4
The Parade *LWTH* * SG6 13 E4
Parishes Md *STVGE* SG2 36 C5
Park Cl *BLDK* SG7 20 B1
STVGE SG2 40 A3
Park Crs *BLDK* SG7 20 B1
Park Dr *BLDK* SG7 20 B1
Parker Cl *LWTH* SG6 18 D4
Parker's Fld *STVGE* SG2 36 B5
Park Farm Cl *HNLW* SG16 5 E2
Parkfield *LWTH* SG6 20 A4
Park Gdns *BLDK* SG7 20 B1
Park Ga *HTCHE/RSTV* SG4 23 G5
Park La *HNLW* SG16 5 E1
KNEB SG3 42 C2
Park Pl *STVG* SG1 2 D4
Park St *BLDK* SG7 14 B5
HTCHE/RSTV SG4 23 F5
The Park *HERT/WAS* * SG14 45 E1
Park Vw *STVGE* SG2 40 A3
Park Wy *HTCH/STOT* SG5 23 F5
Parkway *STVGE* SG2 39 H3
Parsons Green Est *STVG* * SG1 32 B4
Pascal Wy *LWTH* SG6 19 G1
Passingham Av
HTCHE/RSTV SG4 23 H5
Pasture Rd *LWTH* SG6 18 D5
The Pastures *STVGE* SG2 36 C1
Paynes Cl *LWTH* SG6 13 F4
Payne's Pk *HTCH/STOT* SG5 23 F4
Pearl Ct *BLDK* * SG7 14 C4
Pearsall Cl *LWTH* SG6 19 G3
Pear Tree Cl *HNLW* SG16 10 C3
Pear Tree Dell *LWTH* SG6 25 G1
Peartree Wy *STVGE* SG2 3 K7
Pelican Wy *LWTH* SG6 13 E4
Pembroke Rd *BLDK* SG7 14 C5
Penfold Cl *BLDK* SG7 20 D1
Penn Rd *STVG* SG1 2 E4
Penn Wy *LWTH* SG6 19 G5
Pennyfather Cl *KNEB* SG3 44 D5
Peppercorn Wk
HTCHE/RSTV SG4 24 A4
Pepsal End *STVGE* SG2 40 A3
Pepys Wy *BLDK* SG7 14 A5
Periwinkle La *HTCH/STOT* SG5 23 G2
Peters Wy *KNEB* SG3 43 G1
Petworth Cl *STVGE* SG2 40 B5
Pike End *STVG* SG1 2 D1
Pilgrims Wy *STVG* SG1 32 A4
Pinewoods *STVGE* * SG2 39 G3
Pinnocks La *BLDK* SG7 20 C1
Pirton Cl *HTCH/STOT* SG5 23 E4
Pirton Rd *HTCH/STOT* SG5 16 B2
HTCH/STOT SG5 22 C4
Pix Ct *ARL/CHE* SG15 5 H2
Pixmore Av *LWTH* SG6 19 G2
Pixmore Est *LWTH* * SG6 19 G2
Pixmore Wy *LWTH* SG6 19 E3
Pix Rd *HTCH/STOT* SG5 6 D5
LWTH SG6 19 F2
Plash Dr *STVG* SG1 2 E3
Plum Tree Rd *HNLW* SG16 10 C2
Pollard Gdns *STVG* SG1 35 G1
Pond Cl *STVG* * SG1 34 D2
Pondcroft Rd *KNEB* SG3 43 H2
Pond La *BLDK* SG7 14 B5
Pondside *HTCHE/RSTV* SG4 30 D2
Poplar Cl *HTCHE/RSTV* SG4 28 D1
The Poplars *ARL/CHE* SG15 5 H2
HTCH/STOT SG5 17 G3
Popple Wy *STVG* SG1 2 E2
Poppy Md *STVG* SG1 3 H5
Portman Cl *HTCH/STOT* SG5 23 E1
Portmill La *HTCH/STOT* SG5 23 G4
Post Office Rw *HTCHE/RSTV* SG4 27 E2
Potters La *STVG* SG1 34 C5
Pound Av *STVG* SG1 2 C1
Pound Ct *STVG* * SG1 2 C1
Prestatyn Cl *STVG* SG1 34 C2
Primary Wy *ARL/CHE* SG15 11 H1
Primett Rd *STVG* SG1 2 B1
Primrose Cl *ARL/CHE* SG15 11 H1
Primrose Ct *STVG* * SG1 35 E2
Primrose Hill Rd *STVG* SG1 35 E2
Primrose La *ARL/CHE* SG15 11 H1
Prince's St *HTCH/STOT* SG5 7 E3
Priory Dell *STVG* SG1 3 F4
Priory End *HTCHE/RSTV* SG4 28 C1
Priory La *HTCHE/RSTV* SG4 30 A2
Priory Vw *HTCHE/RSTV* SG4 29 H2
Priory Wy *HTCHE/RSTV* SG4 28 B2
Protea Wy *LWTH* SG6 19 G2
Providence Gv *STVG* SG1 35 F1
Providence Wy *BLDK* SG7 20 C1
Pryor Rd *BLDK* SG7 20 C1
Pryor Wy *LWTH* SG6 20 A3
Pullman Dr *HTCHE/RSTV* SG4 24 A4
Pulter's Wy *HTCHE/RSTV* SG4 23 H5
Purwell La *HTCHE/RSTV* SG4 24 B3
Pyms Cl *LWTH* SG6 13 G5

Q

The Quadrant *LWTH* SG6 19
STVG SG1 2
Queen Anne's Cl *HTCH/STOT* SG5 7
Queen St *HTCH/STOT* SG5 7
HTCHE/RSTV SG4 23
Queensway *STVG* * SG1 2
Queenswood Dr
HTCHE/RSTV SG4 24
Quills *LWTH* SG6 20
Quinn Wy *LWTH* SG6 19

R

Raban Cl *STVGE* SG2 40
Radburn Wy *LWTH* SG6 19
Radcliffe Rd *HTCH/STOT* SG5 23
Radwell La *BLDK* SG7 13
Raffin Cl *KNEB* SG3 44
Raffin Green La *KNEB* SG3 44
Raffin Pk *KNEB* SG3 44
Raleigh Crs *STVGE* SG2 35
The Rally *ARL/CHE* SG15 5
Ramerick Gdns *ARL/CHE* SG15 11
Ramsdell *STVG* SG1 3
Randals Hl *STVGE* SG2 40
Rand's Meadow *HTCH/STOT* SG5 16
Ransom Cl *HTCHE/RSTV* SG4 28
Ranworth Av *STVGE* SG2 40
Rectory La *KNEB* SG3 44
STVG SG1 30
Redcar Dr *STVG* SG1 34
Redhill Rd *HTCH/STOT* SG5 22
Redhoods Wy East *LWTH* SG6 18
Redhoods Wy West *LWTH* SG6 18
Redlands *BLDK* * SG7 15
Redoubt Cl *HTCHE/RSTV* SG4 23
Redwing Cl *STVGE* SG2 36
Regent Ct *HTCH/STOT* SG5 7
Regent St *HTCH/STOT* SG5 7
Rhee Spring *BLDK* SG7 15
Riccat La *STVG* SG1 31
The Rickyard Norton Hall Farm
LWTH * SG6 13
Riddell Gdns *BLDK* SG7 14
Riddy Hill Cl *HTCHE/RSTV* * SG4 23
Ridge Av *LWTH* SG6 19
Ridge Rd *LWTH* SG6 19
Ridgeway *STVG* SG1 3
The Ridgeway *HTCH/STOT* SG5 23
The Ridings *STVGE* SG2 40
Ridlins End *STVGE* SG2 40
Ringtale Pl *BLDK* SG7 15
Ripon Rd *STVG* SG1 31
The Rise *BLDK* SG7 20
River Ct *HTCH/STOT* SG5 17
River Md *HTCH/STOT* SG5 22
Rivett Cl *BLDK* SG7 14
Rockingham Wy *STVG* SG1 3
Roebuck Ct *STVGE* SG2 39
Roebuck Ga *STVGE* SG2 39
Roe Cl *HTCH/STOT* SG5 6
Roman La *BLDK* SG7 14
Romany Cl *LWTH* SG6 18
Rookery Yd *STVG* SG1 34
Rookes Cl *LWTH* SG6 19
Rook Tree Cl *HTCH/STOT* * SG5 7
Rook Tree La *HTCH/STOT* SG5 7
Rookwood Dr *STVGE* SG2 40
Rosemont Cl *LWTH* SG6 18
Ross Ct *STVGE* SG2 36
Roundwood Cl *HTCHE/RSTV* SG4 24
Rowan Cl *HTCHE/RSTV* SG4 27
Rowan Crs *LWTH* SG6 18
STVG SG1 35
Rowan Gv *HTCHE/RSTV* SG4 28
The Rowans *BLDK* SG7 2
Rowland Rd *STVG* SG1 3
Rowland Wy *LWTH* SG6 19
Royston Rd *BLDK* SG7 14
Ruckles Cl *STVG* SG1 3
Rudd Cl *STVGE* SG2 40
Rudham Gv *LWTH* SG6 19
Rundells *LWTH* SG6 20
Runnalow *LWTH* SG6 1
Rushby Md *LWTH* SG6 1
Rushby Pl *LWTH* SG6 19
Rushby Wk *LWTH* SG6 19
Ruskin La *HTCHE/RSTV* SG4 2
Russell Cl *STVGE* SG2 4
Rutherford Cl *STVG* SG1 3
Ryder Av *HTCH/STOT* SG5 1
Ryecroft *STVG* SG1 3

'e Gdns BLDK SG7 15 E4
ley Cl HNLW SG16 4 C5

S

ddlers Cl BLDK SG7 14 B5
ffron Cl ARL/CHE SG15 5 H3
ffron Hl LWTH SG6 18 D2
Albans Dr STVG SG1 31 F5
Albans Link STVG SG1 31 F5
Andrews Dr STVG SG1 31 G3
Andrew's Pl HTCHE/RSTV SG4 23 G5
Anne's Rd HTCH/STOT SG5 23 G3
Augustine Cl HTCH/STOT SG5 23 G3
Davids Cl STVG SG1 31 G3
Elmo Ct HTCHE/RSTV * SG4 28 C1
Faiths Cl HTCHE/RSTV SG4 24 A2
George's Wy STVG SG1 2 D4
Giles Rd HTCHE/RSTV SG4 42 A5
John's Rd ARL/CHE SG15 11 H1
HTCHE/RSTV SG4 28 C1
Katharines Cl HTCH/STOT SG5 17 E5
Margarets STVGE SG2 39 G2
Martin's Rd KNEB SG3 43 H2
Mary's Av HTCH/STOT SG5 7 E4
Mary's Cl LWTH SG6 25 E1
STVGE SG2 40 D2
Mary's Wy BLDK SG7 20 B2
Michael's Mt HTCHE/RSTV SG4 23 H3
Michaels Rd HTCHE/RSTV SG4 24 A3
Olives HTCH/STOT SG5 6 D4
Peter's Av ARL/CHE SG15 5 H3
e Dr BLDK SG7 14 C4
isbury Rd BLDK SG7 14 B4
STVG SG1 31 H4
ly Deards La WLYN AL6 42 C3
nderling Cl LWTH SG6 12 D5
ndover Cl HTCHE/RSTV SG4 24 A5
ndown Rd STVG SG1 32 B5
ndy Gv HTCHE/RSTV SG4 23 G5
nfoine Cl HTCHE/RSTV SG4 24 B3
unders Cl LWTH SG6 19 G1
xon Av HTCH/STOT SG5 7 E2
xon Cl LWTH SG6 13 E4
xon Wy BLDK SG7 15 E4
yer Wy KNEB SG3 43 G3
arborough Av STVG SG1 34 B2
ool Cl STVGE SG2 40 A1
oolfields LWTH SG6 19 H3
ool La HTCHE/RSTV SG4 27 F2
TVGE SG2 40 D2
ool Wk LWTH SG6 19 G2
ott Rd STVGE SG2 36 A2
ond Av LWTH SG6 19 H2
ebohm Cl HTCH/STOT SG5 22 D2
ton Rd STVG SG1 32 A5
ate Pl STVG SG1 32 A4
pentine Cl STVG SG1 32 B4
ackledell STVGE SG2 39 G2
ackleton Spring STVGE SG2 39 H1
arps Wy HTCHE/RSTV SG4 23 H3
arwater Cl STVGE SG2 36 C5
eepcroft Hl STVGE SG2 40 C1
elley Cl HTCHE/RSTV SG4 24 B4
ephall Gn STVGE SG2 40 A2
ephall La STVGE SG2 39 G3
ephall Vw STVG SG1 3 J3
ephall Wy STVGE SG2 36 A5
epherds La STVG SG1 34 A3
epherds Md HTCH/STOT SG5 23 F1
ringham Av STVG SG1 30 C5
rwood LWTH SG6 13 E5
ley Cl STVGE SG2 36 A1
reham Cl STVG SG1 34 B1
rt La STVGE SG2 36 D5
tt La LWTH SG6 19 F2
cut Rd HTCHE/RSTV SG4 29 H2
dons Rd STVGE SG2 36 B3
m Rd STVG SG1 2 E4
erbirch Av HTCH/STOT SG5 7 E2
pson Dr BLDK SG7 14 C5
ield Cl STVG SG1 3 J3
Cl STVG SG1 2 D1
La STVG SG1 2 C1
on Cl STVGE SG2 40 B2
Hills Rbt STVG SG1 2 C6
Hills Wy STVG SG1 2 A7
n Av LWTH SG6 19 H2
gness Rd STVG SG1 34 B1
ton Cl STVGE SG2 39 G4
ark Cnr STVGE SG2 40 C1
ps Hyde STVGE SG2 40 B3
La KNEB SG3 42 C2
n Ct STVG SG1 3 H1
lswell La HTCH/STOT SG5 17 F3
Snipe HTCHE/RSTV SG4 26 D2
Sollershott East LWTH SG6 19 E4
Sollershott Hall LWTH * SG6 19 E4
Sollershott West LWTH SG6 18 D4
Sorrel Garth HTCHE/RSTV SG4 23 H5
Souberie Av LWTH SG6 19 E3
South Cl BLDK SG7 20 C1
Southend Cl STVG SG1 34 D2
Southern Av HNLW SG16 10 C2
Southern Wy LWTH SG6 12 D5
Southfields LWTH SG6 13 E4
Southgate STVG SG1 2 D5
South Hill Cl HTCHE/RSTV * SG4 23 H5
South Pl HTCH/STOT SG5 23 E3
South Rd BLDK SG7 20 C1
Southsea Rd STVG SG1 34 C1
South Vw LWTH SG6 19 E3
Southwark Cl STVG SG1 32 A5
Sparhawke LWTH SG6 13 F4
Sparrow Dr STVGE SG2 36 B5
Speke Cl STVGE * SG2 36 C4
Spellbrooke HTCH/STOT SG5 23 E3
Sperberry Hl HTCHE/RSTV SG4 29 E4
Spinney La WLYN AL6 43 E5
The Spinney BLDK SG7 20 B1
STVGE SG2 36 C2
Spreckley Cl HNLW SG16 4 C5
Spring Dr STVGE SG2 39 H4
Spring Rd LWTH SG6 18 D3
Springshott LWTH SG6 18 D3
Spurrs Cl HTCHE/RSTV SG4 24 A4
The Spur STVG SG1 3 F5
Standhill Cl HTCHE/RSTV SG4 23 G5
Standhill Rd HTCHE/RSTV SG4 23 G5
Stane Fld LWTH SG6 19 G5
Stane St BLDK SG7 14 D4
Stanley Rd STVGE SG2 36 A2
Stanmore Rd STVG SG1 34 D2
Station Ap HTCHE/RSTV SG4 23 H3
KNEB SG3 43 G2
Station Pl LWTH SG6 19 E2
Station Rd ARL/CHE SG15 11 H1
BLDK SG7 14 C4
HNLW SG16 10 A1
KNEB SG3 43 G2
LWTH SG6 19 E2
Station Wy LWTH SG6 18 D2
Stevenage Rd HTCHE/RSTV SG4 28 C1
KNEB SG3 39 G5
STVGE SG2 37 E1
Stirling Cl HTCHE/RSTV * SG4 24 B4
STVGE SG2 40 B5
Stobarts Cl KNEB SG3 43 G1
Stockens Dell KNEB SG3 43 G3
Stockens Gn KNEB SG3 43 G3
Stonecroft KNEB SG3 43 G2
Stoneley LWTH SG6 13 E4
Stonnells Cl LWTH SG6 13 E5
Stony Cft STVG SG1 2 E2
Storehouse La HTCHE/RSTV SG4 23 G5
Stormont Rd HTCH/STOT SG5 23 G2
Stotfold Rd ARL/CHE SG15 5 H2
BLDK SG7 7 H2
LWTH SG6 18 B1
Strafford Ct KNEB SG3 43 H2
Strathmore Av HTCH/STOT SG5 23 F2
Straw Plait ARL/CHE SG15 11 G1
Stringers La STVGE SG2 40 D3
Stuart Dr HTCHE/RSTV SG4 24 A4
Sturgeon's Wy HTCHE/RSTV SG4 24 A1
Sturrock Wy HTCHE/RSTV SG4 24 B5
Such Cl LWTH SG6 19 G1
Sunnyside Rd HTCHE/RSTV SG4 23 H5
Sun St BLDK SG7 14 B5
HTCH/STOT SG5 23 F5
Sutcliffe Cl STVG SG1 35 H1
Swangley's La KNEB SG3 43 H2
Swanstand LWTH SG6 20 A4
Sweyns Md STVGE SG2 36 B1
Swift Cl LWTH SG6 12 D5
Swinburne Av HTCH/STOT SG5 22 D2
Swingate STVG SG1 2 C4
Sycamore Cl HTCHE/RSTV SG4 28 D2
The Sycamores BLDK SG7 14 B4
Symonds Green La STVG SG1 34 B2
Symonds Green Rd STVG SG1 34 B2
Symonds Rd HTCH/STOT SG5 23 E3

T

Tabbs Cl LWTH SG6 13 G5
Tacitus Cl STVGE SG2 36 B1
Talbot St HTCH/STOT SG5 23 E3
Talbot Wy LWTH SG6 13 G5
Talisman St HTCHE/RSTV SG4 24 B4
Tall Trees HTCHE/RSTV SG4 28 D2
Tamar Cl STVG SG1 31 H3
Tatlers La STVGE SG2 36 C4
Taylor's Rd HTCH/STOT SG5 7 E2
Taywood Cl STVGE SG2 40 A2
Tedder Av HNLW SG16 4 C5
Telford Av STVGE SG2 36 A4
Templar Av BLDK SG7 20 C2
Temple Ct BLDK * SG7 20 C2
Temple Gdns LWTH * SG6 13 H5
The Tene BLDK SG7 14 C5
Tennyson Av HTCHE/RSTV SG4 24 B4
Thatchers End HTCHE/RSTV SG4 24 C3
Third Av LWTH SG6 19 H1
Thirlmere STVG SG1 32 B4
Thistley La HTCHE/RSTV SG4 28 C4
Thornbury Cl STVGE SG2 39 H4
Three Star Pk HNLW * SG16 10 C2
Thristers Cl LWTH * SG6 19 G5
Thurlow Cl STVG SG1 31 E5
Thurnall Cl BLDK SG7 14 C5
Tilehouse St HTCH/STOT SG5 23 F4
Tillers Link STVGE SG2 39 H2
Times Cl HTCH/STOT SG5 23 E1
Tintern Cl KNEB SG3 39 H5
Tippet Ct STVG SG1 2 D7
Tippett Ct STVG * SG1 2 D7
Titmus Cl STVG SG1 3 F1
Torquay Crs STVG SG1 34 C2
Totts La STVGE SG2 33 H5
Tower Cl HTCHE/RSTV SG4 30 A3
The Towers STVG SG1 2 D5
Towers Rd STVG SG1 2 D5
Townley LWTH SG6 19 H4
Town Sq STVG SG1 2 D4
Trafford Cl STVG SG1 31 F5
Traherne Cl HTCHE/RSTV SG4 28 C1
Trajan Ga STVG SG1 32 C5
Trent Cl STVG SG1 31 F5
Trevor Rd HTCHE/RSTV SG4 23 H3
Trigg Ter STVG SG1 3 F1
Trinity Pl STVG SG1 2 C1
Trinity Rd HTCH/STOT SG5 6 D3
STVG SG1 2 B1
Tristram Rd HTCHE/RSTV SG4 23 H1
Truemans Rd HTCH/STOT SG5 23 E1
Trumper Rd STVG SG1 35 G1
Truro Ct STVG * SG1 31 G4
Tudor Cl STVG SG1 30 D5
Tudor Ct HTCH/STOT SG5 23 E5
Turf La HTCHE/RSTV SG4 30 C2
Turner Cl STVG SG1 30 D4
Turnpike La HTCH/STOT SG5 17 E5
Turpin's Ri STVGE SG2 39 F3
Turpin's Wy BLDK SG7 20 C1
Twinwoods STVG SG1 3 H5
The Twitchell BLDK SG7 14 C5
Tye End STVGE SG2 40 A4

U

Ullswater Cl STVG SG1 32 B4
Underwood Rd STVG SG1 30 D4
Unwin Cl LWTH SG6 18 D4
Unwin Pl STVGE SG2 40 B1
Unwin Rd STVGE SG2 40 B1
Uplands STVGE SG2 36 C1
Uplands Av HTCHE/RSTV SG4 24 A5
Upper Maylins LWTH SG6 19 H4
Upper Sean STVGE SG2 39 H1
Upperstone Cl HTCH/STOT SG5 7 E4
Upper Tilehouse St
HTCH/STOT SG5 23 E5

V

Valerian Wy STVGE SG2 36 C1
Vallansgate STVGE SG2 40 A3
Valley Rd LWTH SG6 18 C1
Valley Wy STVGE SG2 39 G2
Vardon Rd STVG SG1 35 G1
Vaughan Rd HTCH/STOT SG5 6 D4
Venables Ter STVG * SG1 34 D2
Verity Wy STVG SG1 31 H5
Verulam Rd HTCH/STOT SG5 23 G3
Vicarage Cl ARL/CHE SG15 5 H2
Victoria Cl STVG SG1 35 E2
Victoria Wy HTCH/STOT SG5 23 E3
Village St HTCHE/RSTV SG4 38 A3
Vincent LWTH SG6 19 H4
Vinters Av STVG SG1 3 G4

W

Wadnall Wy KNEB SG3 43 G3
Walden End STVG SG1 2 E5
Walkern Rd HERT/WAS SG14 45 H1
STVG SG1 35 E1
STVGE SG2 37 F5
Wallace Wy HTCHE/RSTV SG4 17 H5
Wallington Rd BLDK SG7 14 D5
Walnut Av BLDK SG7 20 D1
Walnut Cl HTCH/STOT SG5 7 E4
HTCHE/RSTV SG4 23 H5
Walnut Tree Cl STVGE SG2 36 C5
Walnut Wy HTCH/STOT SG5 17 F4
Walsham Cl STVGE SG2 40 B5
Walsh Cl HTCH/STOT SG5 23 E4
Walsworth Rd HTCHE/RSTV SG4 23 H4
Waltham Rd HTCHE/RSTV SG4 23 G5
Wansbeck Cl STVG SG1 31 H3
Warners Cl STVGE SG2 40 A1
Warren Cl LWTH SG6 18 C1
Warren La BLDK SG7 21 E1
Warrensgreen La
HTCHE/RSTV SG4 32 C1
Warwick Rd STVGE SG2 36 B3
Watercress Cl STVGE SG2 36 C4
Waterdell La HTCHE/RSTV SG4 28 C4
Water La HTCH/STOT SG5 23 G2
Waterloo La HTCH/STOT SG5 16 B2
Waters End HTCH/STOT SG5 6 D4
Watton Rd KNEB SG3 43 H2
Waverley Cl STVGE SG2 39 H4
Waysbrook LWTH SG6 19 G4
Waysmeet LWTH SG6 19 F4
Weavers Wy BLDK SG7 14 D5
Webb Cl LWTH SG6 19 H3
Webb Ri STVG SG1 35 G2
Wedgewood Cl
HTCHE/RSTV SG4 24 B4
Wedgewood Ct * STVG SG1 32 B3
Wedgewood Pk STVG SG1 32 B4
Wedgewood Rd
HTCHE/RSTV SG4 24 A4
Wedgwood Ct STVG SG1 32 B4
Wedgwood Ga STVG SG1 32 A4
Wedgwood Wy STVG SG1 32 A4
Wedmore Rd HTCHE/RSTV SG4 23 H5
Wedon Wy BLDK SG7 15 F1
Weedon Cl HNLW SG16 4 D5
Wellingham Av HTCH/STOT SG5 23 E2
Wellington Rd STVGE SG2 36 B4
Wesley Cl ARL/CHE SG15 11 H1
West Aly HTCH/STOT SG5 23 F4
West Av BLDK SG7 14 B5
Westbury Cl HTCH/STOT SG5 22 D3
Westbury Pl LWTH SG6 18 D3
West Cl HTCHE/RSTV SG4 24 A1
STVG SG1 3 G3
West Dr ARL/CHE SG15 11 H1
Westell Cl BLDK SG7 14 D5
Western Av HNLW SG16 10 C2
Western Cl LWTH SG6 12 D4
Western Wy LWTH SG6 12 D4
Westfield Cl HTCH/STOT SG5 23 E4
Westfield La HTCH/STOT SG5 23 E4
Westfield Rd HNLW SG16 4 D1
West Ga STVG SG1 2 D4
West Hl HTCH/STOT SG5 23 E4
Westholme LWTH SG6 13 E5
Westland Rd KNEB SG3 43 H2
Westmill La HTCH/STOT SG5 22 D1
Westmill Lawns HTCH/STOT SG5 23 E2
Westmill Rd HTCH/STOT SG5 22 D1
Weston Rd STVG SG1 35 F1
Weston Wy BLDK SG7 14 B5
West Reach STVGE SG2 39 G2
West Vw LWTH SG6 18 C4
Westwood Av HTCHE/RSTV SG4 23 H5
Wetherby Cl STVG SG1 36 B1
Wheat Hl LWTH SG6 18 D1
Wheatlands STVGE SG2 36 B2
Whinbush Gv HTCH/STOT SG5 23 G3
Whinbush Rd HTCH/STOT SG5 23 G4
Whitechurch Gdns LWTH SG6 19 H5
White Crofts HTCH/STOT SG5 6 D3
Whitegale Cl HTCHE/RSTV SG4 23 H5
Whitehicks LWTH SG6 13 F4
White Hl STVGE SG2 33 H3
Whitehill Cl HTCHE/RSTV * SG4 23 H5
Whitehill Rd HTCHE/RSTV SG4 23 H5
Whitehorse St BLDK SG7 14 C5
Whitehurst Av HTCH/STOT SG5 23 G2
Whitesmead Rd STVG SG1 35 F2
Whitethorn La LWTH SG6 19 F5
The White Wy STVGE SG2 36 B2
Whitney Dr STVG SG1 30 D5

Whittington La *STVG* SG1 ....3 F6
Whittle Cl *HNLW* SG16 ....10 C1
Whitworth Jones Av *HNLW* SG16 ....4 D5
Whitworth Rd *STVG* SG1 ....32 A3
Whomerley Rd *STVG* SG1 ....3 F6
Wickfield *KNEB* * SG3....43 H5
Wickfield Cl *KNEB* SG3....43 H5
Wigram Wy *STVGE* SG2 ....36 A5
Wilbury Cl *LWTH* SG6 ....18 B1
Wilbury Hills Rd *LWTH* SG6 ....18 B2
Wilbury Rd *LWTH* SG6 ....18 C1
Wilbury Wy *HTCHE/RSTV* SG4....17 H5
Wildwood La *STVG* SG1 ....3 F6
William Pl *STVGE* SG2 ....39 H1
Willian Church Rd *LWTH* SG6 ....25 F1
Willian Rd *HTCHE/RSTV* SG4 ....24 A2
Willian Wy *BLDK* SG7 ....20 B2
LWTH SG6 ....19 F4
Willoughby Wy
HTCHE/RSTV SG4....23 H5
Willow La *HTCH/STOT* SG5....22 D5
Willows Link *STVGE* SG2 ....39 H3
The Willows *HTCHE/RSTV* SG4 ....28 D1
STVGE SG2 ....39 H4
Willow Tree Wy *HTCH/STOT* SG5 ....23 F1
Wilshere Crs *HTCHE/RSTV* SG4 ....24 B3
Wilson Cl *STVG* SG1....31 E5
Wilsons Cl *STVG* * SG1 ....31 E5
Wilton Rd *HTCH/STOT* SG5 ....23 F2
Wiltshire Rd *STVGE* SG2....3 K6
Winchester Cl *STVG* SG1 ....31 H4
Windermere Cl *STVG* SG1 ....32 C4
Windmill Hl *HTCHE/RSTV* SG4....23 G4
Windsor Cl *STVGE* SG2 ....40 A5
Winston Cl *HTCH/STOT* SG5....23 E4
Winters La *STVGE* SG2 ....33 G5
Winton Cl *LWTH* SG6....13 H5
Wisden Rd *STVG* SG1 ....35 G1
Witter Av *HTCH/STOT* SG5....17 F4
Woburn Cl *STVGE* SG2 ....40 B5
Wolvescroft *KNEB* * SG3 ....43 H5
Wolves Mere *KNEB* SG3....43 H5
Woodcock Rd *STVGE* SG2 ....40 C2
Wood Dr *STVGE* SG2....40 A2
Woodfield Rd *STVG* SG1 ....30 D5
Woodhurst *LWTH* SG6 ....13 E5
Woodlands Meade
HTCHE/RSTV SG4....27 E3
Woodland Wy *BLDK* SG7 ....20 C2
STVGE SG2 ....39 H3
Woodstock *KNEB* SG3 ....43 G4
Woolgrove Rd *HTCHE/RSTV* SG4 ....23 H2
Woolners Wy *STVG* SG1 ....2 A1
Woolston Av *LWTH* SG6....19 F4
Works Rd *LWTH* SG6....19 G1
Worsdell Wy *HTCHE/RSTV* SG4....24 A4
Wortham Wy *STVGE* SG2....40 A1
Wratten Cl *HTCH/STOT* SG5....23 F5
Wratten Rd East
HTCH/STOT SG5 ....23 F5
Wratten Rd West
HTCH/STOT SG5 ....23 E5
Wrayfields *HTCH/STOT* SG5 ....7 G3
Wren Cl *STVGE* SG2....36 A3
Wrights Meadow *STVGE* SG2 ....37 G1
Wrights Orch *STVGE* SG2....40 D2
Wyatt Cl *HTCH/STOT* SG5....17
Wychdell *STVGE* SG2 40
Wych Elm La *KNEB* SG3 43
Wycklond Cl *HTCH/STOT* * SG5....6
Wymondley Cl *HTCHE/RSTV* SG4 23
Wymondley Rd
HTCHE/RSTV SG4....23
Wynn Cl *BLDK* SG7 14
Wyrley Dell *LWTH* SG6 19

Yardley *LWTH* SG6 19
Yarmouth Rd *STVG* SG1....34
Yeomanry Dr *BLDK* SG7....14
Yeomans Dr *STVGE* SG2....40
York Rd *HTCH/STOT* SG5 23
STVG SG1....31

Index - featured places

Algrey Trading Estate
HTCHE/RSTV SG4 .... 23 H2
Almond Hill School
STVG SG1 .... 35 E1
Arlesey FC
ARL/CHE SG15.... 11 H2
Ascot Industrial Estate
LWTH SG6.... 19 G1
Ashley Business Centre
HTCH/STOT SG5 .... 23 G3
Ashtree Primary School
STVGE SG2 .... 36 B5
Ashville Trading Estate
BLDK SG7 .... 14 C4
Aston St Marys Primary School
STVGE SG2 .... 40 D1
Baldock Health Centre
BLDK SG7 .... 20 C1
Baldock Industrial Estate
BLDK SG7 .... 20 C1
Bancroft Business Centre
HTCH/STOT SG5 .... 23 G3
Barclay School
STVG SG1 .... 35 E1
Barnwell School
STVGE SG2 .... 40 A2
Bedwell Community Centre
STVG SG1 .... 3 H4
Bedwell Medical Centre
STVG SG1 .... 3 J3
Bedwell Primary School
STVG SG1 .... 3 J2
Bells House Gallery
LWTH SG6.... 19 E2
Blue Gold Trading Estate
ARL/CHE SG15 .... 5 H5
Bondor Business Centre
BLDK SG7 .... 20 B1
Bowmans Trading Estate
STVG SG1 .... 34 C4
Brandles School
BLDK SG7 .... 20 B1
Bridger Packaging FC
LWTH SG6.... 19 E5
Broom Barns JMI School
STVG SG1 .... 3 F5
Burydale Junior School
STVGE SG2 .... 40 A3
Business East Obsdoc House Centre
LWTH SG6.... 19 H2
Business & Technology Centre
STVG SG1 .... 34 C4
Canary Club FC
HTCH/STOT SG5 .... 23 F3
Chesfield Downs Golf Club
HTCHE/RSTV SG4 .... 26 A4
Churchgate Shopping Centre
HTCH/STOT SG5 .... 23 F4
Cineworld Cinema
STVG SG1 .... 2 B5
Collenswood School
STVGE SG2 .... 36 B5
Court Street Register Office
STVG SG1 .... 2 C4
Covered Market
STVG SG1 .... 2 D4
Datchworth School
KNEB SG3.... 44 C4
Derwent Lower School
HNLW SG16 .... 4 C5
Diamond Industrial Centre
LWTH SG6.... 19 H1
Fairfield Hospital
HTCH/STOT SG5 .... 12 B3
Fairlands Primary School
STVG SG1 .... 2 D1
Family Leisure Centre
STVG SG1 .... 2 C4
Fearnhill School
LWTH SG6.... 18 B3
Fearnhill Sports Centre
LWTH SG6.... 18 B3
Featherstone Wood Primary School
STVGE SG2 .... 40 B1
The Forum Retail Park
STVG SG1 .... 2 C3
The Giles Infant & Junior School
STVG SG1 .... 31 G5
Gordon Craig Centre Cinema
STVG SG1 .... 2 B4
Gothic Mede Lower School
ARL/CHE SG15.... 5 H5
Grange Junior School
LWTH SG6.... 13 E3
Graveley Primary School
HTCHE/RSTV SG4 .... 30 C2
Green Lane Industrial Estate
LWTH SG6.... 19 G1
Greenside Special School
STVGE SG2 .... 39 H2
Gunnels Wood Industrial Estate
STVG SG1 .... 39 E1
Hartsfield Primary School
BLDK SG7 .... 14 C5
Harwood Park Crematorium
KNEB SG3.... 44 B1
Heathcote School
STVGE SG2 .... 39 H2
Henlow Airfield
HNLW SG16 .... 4 B3
Henlow Industrial Estate
HNLW SG16 .... 10 C1
Henlow Middle School
HNLW SG16 .... 5 F1
Highbury Infant School
HTCHE/RSTV SG4 .... 23 G5
Highfield School
LWTH SG6.... 18 C5
Highover JMI School
HTCHE/RSTV SG4 .... 24 B2
Hill Shott Infant School
LWTH SG6.... 19 F2
Hitchin Boys School
HTCH/STOT SG5 .... 23 F3
The Hitchin Business Centre
HTCHE/RSTV SG4 .... 17 H4
Hitchin Cricket Club
HTCH/STOT SG5 .... 22 D4
Hitchin Girls School
HTCHE/RSTV SG4 .... 23 G4
Hitchin Road Industrial & Business Centre
ARL/CHE SG15.... 11 G2
Hitchin Swimming Pool
HTCH/STOT SG5 .... 23 F3
Hollywood Bowl
STVG SG1 .... 2 A5
Hyatt Trading Estate
STVG SG1 .... 34 B4
Icknield Infant School
LWTH SG6.... 18 C2
John Henry Newman RC School
STVG SG1 .... 30 C5
Jubilee Trading Estate
LWTH SG6.... 19 H1
Kingshott School
HTCHE/RSTV SG4 .... 29 E1
Knebworth Golf Club
KNEB SG3.... 43 G1
Knebworth House, Gardens & Country Park
KNEB SG3.... 42 C1
Knebworth Physiotherapy Clinic
STVGE SG2 .... 40 B5
Knights Templar School
BLDK SG7 .... 14 B5
Knowl Piece
HTCHE/RSTV SG4 .... 17 H5
Lannock Primary School
LWTH SG6.... 19 H4
Larwood School
STVG SG1 .... 35 G2
Letchmore Infant School
STVG SG1 .... 35 E2
Letchworth Business Centre
LWTH SG6.... 19 H2
Letchworth Garden City FC
LWTH SG6.... 19 H3
Letchworth Golf Club
LWTH SG6.... 25 E1
Letchworth Museum & Art Gallery
LWTH SG6.... 19 E3
Letchworth Swimming Pool
LWTH SG6.... 19 F1
Leys Primary School
STVG SG1 .... 31 H4
Lister Hospital
STVG SG1 .... 30 C4
Lodge Farm Primary School
STVGE SG2 .... 36 B2
Long Meadow Infant & Junior School
STVGE SG2 .... 40 A3
Lonsdale School
STVG SG1 .... 35 G2
Lordship Gardens
STVGE SG2 .... 37 H5
Marquis Business Centre
BLDK SG7 .... 14 D4
Marriotts School
STVGE SG2 .... 3 K2
Martins Wood Primary School
STVG SG1 .... 32 A5
Mary Exton Primary School
HTCHE/RSTV SG4 .... 24 B4
Marymead Industrial Estate
STVGE SG2 .... 40 A4
Megabowl
STVG SG1 .... 39 E1
Monkswood Retail Park
STVG SG1 .... 2 E7
Moss Bury Primary School
STVG SG1 .... 35 H2
Mount Pleasant Golf Club
HNLW SG16 10
Natural Art Gallery & Science Pictures
HTCH/STOT SG5 23
Nobel School
STVGE SG2 36
Northfields Infant School
LWTH SG6.... 13
North Hertfordshire College
LWTH SG6.... 19
North Hertfordshire College of Further Education
HTCHE/RSTV SG4 24
North Hertfordshire College, Stevenage Centre
STVG SG1 2
North Hertfordshire Leisure Centre
LWTH SG6.... 19
North Hertfordshire Secondary Centre
LWTH SG6.... 18
Norton St Nicholas Primary School
LWTH SG6.... 13
Norton School
LWTH SG6.... 13
Nup End Industrial Estate
WLYN AL6.... 42
Oakfield Business Corner
LWTH SG6.... 19
Old Oak Close Industrial Estate
ARL/CHE SG15.... 5
Oughtonhead Common Nature Reserve
HTCH/STOT SG5 22
Oughton Primary School
HTCH/STOT SG5 22
Peckworth Industrial Estate
HNLW SG16 10
Pinehill Hospital
HTCHE/RSTV SG4 24
Pin Green Industrial Estate
STVG SG1 32
Pin Green Primary School
STVG SG1 3
Pirton Cross
HTCH/STOT SG5 22
Pixmore Junior School
LWTH SG6.... 19
Portland Industrial Estate
ARL/CHE SG15.... 11
Priory School
HTCH/STOT SG5 23
The Priory
HTCH/STOT SG5 23
Purwell Primary School
HTCHE/RSTV SG4 24
Queen Mother Theatre
HTCHE/RSTV SG4 23
Radburn Primary School
LWTH SG6.... 19
Ridlins Wood Athletics Track
STVGE SG2 40
Roaring Meg Retail Park
STVG SG1 39
Roebuck JMI School
STVGE SG2 39

ebuck Retail Park
STVGE SG2 .... **39** F2
ecroft School
HTCH/STOT SG5 .... **7** F4
und Diamond
Primary School
STVG SG1 .... **36** A1
Andrews CE Primary School
HTCHE/RSTV SG4 .... **23** H4
Christophers School
LWTH SG6.......... **19** E5
Francis College
LWTH SG6.......... **18** D4
Ippolyts Primary School
HTCHE/RSTV SG4 .... **29** E3
Johns RC Primary School
BLDK SG7 .... **20** C1
Margaret Clitherow
RC Primary School
STVGE SG2 .... **39** G2
Marys Junior & Infant School
BLDK SG7 .... **20** B2
Marys Lower School
HTCH/STOT SG5 .... **7** F4
Nicholas Health Centre
STVG SG1 .... **31** G4
Nicholas Recreation Centre
STVG SG1 .... **32** A3
St Thomas More RC
Primary School
LWTH SG6.......... **18** C4
Shaftesbury Industrial Centre
LWTH SG6.......... **19** G1
Shephall Green Infant School
STVGE SG2 .... **40** A2
Southgate Health Centre
STVG SG1 .... **2** C5
Stanmore Road Health Centre
STVG SG1 .... **34** D2
Stevenage Borough FC
STVG SG1 .... **2** D4
Stevenage Business Park
STVG SG1 .... **30** C5
Stevenage Business Park
STVG SG1 .... **32** B4
Stevenage Cricket Club
STVG SG1 .... **2** C2
Stevenage Golf Centre
STVGE SG2 .... **40** D3
Stevenage Leisure Centre
STVG SG1 .... **2** C4
Stevenage Leisure Park
STVG SG1 .... **2** A5
Stevenage Mosque
STVG SG1 .... **35** E2
Stevenage Museum
STVG SG1 .... **2** E4
Stevenage St Nicholas CE
Primary School
STVG SG1 .... **3** H6
Stondon Museum &
Garden Centre
HNLW SG16 .... **10** A2
Stonehill Primary School
LWTH SG6.......... **12** D4
Stotfold Health Centre
HTCH/STOT SG5 .... **6** D4
Strathmore Infant School
HTCH/STOT SG5 .... **23** F1
The Symonds Green
Health Centre
STVG SG1 .... **34** B2
Thomas Alleyne School
STVG SG1 .... **34** D1
Trotts Hill Primary School
STVG SG1 .... **31** G5
Trust Industrial Estate
HTCHE/RSTV SG4 .... **17** H5
Wedgewood Gate
Industrial Estate
STVG SG1 .... **32** A4
Westbury Primary School
LWTH SG6.......... **18** D3
Westgate Centre
STVG SG1 .... **2** C3
Weston Primary School
HTCHE/RSTV SG4 .... **27** F2
Whitehill Junior School
HTCHE/RSTV SG4 .... **28** D1
Wilbury Junior School
LWTH SG6.......... **18** D2
William Ransom JMI School
HTCHE/RSTV SG4 .... **24** A4
Wilshere Dacre Junior School
HTCH/STOT SG5 .... **23** F3
Woodside Industrial Park
LWTH SG6.......... **19** G1
Woolenwick Junior &
Infant School
STVG SG1 .... **34** C3
Woolgrove Special School
LWTH SG6.......... **20** A3
Wymondley Primary School
HTCHE/RSTV SG4 .... **29** G2

Notes